5-2 0

2b L

Sensory and Noetic Consciousness

*International Library of Philosophy
and Scientific Method*

Editor: Ted Honderich

A Catalogue of books already published in the
International Library of Philosophy and Scientific Method
will be found at the end of this volume

FRANZ BRENTANO

Sensory and Noetic Consciousness

Psychology from an Empirical Standpoint III

Edited by
Oskar Kraus

English Edition Edited by
Linda L. McAlister

Translated by
Margarete Schättle and Linda L. McAlister

ROUTLEDGE & KEGAN PAUL

London and Henley

New York: Humanities Press

First published in 1929 as Vom sinnlichen und noetischen Bewußtsein
(Psychologie III) *by Felix Meiner, Leipzig*
This translation first published in 1981
by Routledge & Kegan Paul Ltd
39 Store Street, London WC1E 7DD and
Broadway House, Newtown Road,
Henley-on-Thames, Oxon RG9 1EN
Set in Times 10 on 12 pt by
Computacomp (UK) Ltd Fort William, Scotland
and printed in Great Britain by
Redwood Burn Ltd, Trowbridge & Esher
This translation
© *Routledge & Kegan Paul 1981*

British Library Cataloguing in Publication Data

Brentano, Franz

Sensory and noetic consciousness
– (International library of philosophy
and scientific method).
1. Consciousness – Addresses, essays, lectures
I. Title   II. Kraus, Oskar
III. McAlister, Linda Lee
IV. Series
126   BF311   80–40004

ISBN 0 7100 0404 4

CONTENTS

PREFACE TO THE
ENGLISH EDITION

When Franz Brentano's *Psychologie vom empirischen Standpunkt* appeared in 1874, it consisted of two books, entitled *Psychology as a Science* and *Mental Phenomena in General*, respectively. In Brentano's Foreword to that first edition, he indicated that these were to be merely the first instalments of a larger work which would contain six books altogether. The four which were to follow were to deal in a more detailed way with presentations, judgments, the emotions and acts of will, the relationship between mind and body, and the question of mental life after death. Brentano, however, never fulfilled his promise of four additional volumes of his *Psychology*. This is not to say that he failed to do the philosophical work involved; he was to return to these topics again and again throughout his long career. It has to do in part, rather, with his distaste for the mundane details that go into the preparation of manuscripts for publication. He did the philosophizing, and presented his thoughts, analyses, and conclusions in his classes, but almost no writings on these subjects appeared in print during his lifetime. Another part of the reason why Brentano failed to complete the original project was that his philosophical views were changing and evolving steadily throughout his career. His later philosophical positions were quite different in many respects from those he espoused when he wrote his original *Psychology*, although he retained his general empirical point of view. When, in 1911, Brentano allowed the second book of the *Psychology* to be re-issued under the title *The Classification of Mental Phenomena*, the text was reprinted in its original form because to do otherwise would have required extensive revisions, but many footnotes and a lengthy appendix were added by Brentano so that his mature thinking on the topics touched upon in the *Psychology* would be revealed.

In 1929, eleven years after Brentano's death, his friend and editor, Oskar Kraus, compiled a collection of essays from *Nachlass* on topics relating to psychology. Kraus chose to call this volume *Psychologie III* as though it were the long-awaited third book of Brentano's *Psychology*. In a way, this is how Kraus viewed it. The positions reflected in this volume, however, are those of Brentano's later philosophical period, so the *Psychologie III* really does not constitute a direct continuation of the first two books of *Psychology From an Empirical Standpoint* at all. At best, it is a continuation of the Appendix to *The Classification of Mental Phenomena*. Kraus subtitled his collection *Vom sinnlichen und noetischen Bewusstsein* (*On Sensory and Noetic Consciousness*). In order to avoid the confusing implication of calling this work *Psychologie III*, I have chosen to entitle the English edition *Sensory and Noetic Consciousness* and subtitle it *Psychology III* for purposes of identification.

The present volume is a translation of Oskar Kraus's 1929 collection. It differs only in that I have edited certain portions of Kraus's introductory remarks, especially those of a somewhat polemical nature in which he responds at length to the criticisms of some of his contemporaries, and which would be of interest largely to specialists in the history of early-twentieth-century German philosophy, but not to the general philosophical and psychological readership today. I have also abbreviated some of Kraus's copious footnotes. In each case in which there is an omission, it is indicated in the text by an ellipsis. The present translation was made by me and Professor Margarete Schättle of the Institut für Dolmetschausbildung of the University of Vienna. We would like to express our thanks to Roderick M. Chisholm of Brown University for reading a final draft of the translation and suggesting places where additional work would improve it. The responsibility for any errors that remain is mine.

The translators have, in general, continued the practices used in the English edition of *Psychology From an Empirical Standpoint* when translating certain difficult terms in Brentano's writing. '*Vorstellung*' is sometimes translated as 'presentations', and sometimes as 'idea', or 'thought'. The corresponding verb '*vorstellen*' is translated variously as 'to think of', 'to have before the mind', and as 'to have a presentation of'. '*Anschauung*' is rendered as 'intuition'. '*Als richtig charakterisiert*' is translated as 'experienced as being correct', and, for reasons which

Chisholm sets forth in his Preface to *The True and the Evident*, '*Realia*' is translated as 'things'.

This work is one of a series of translations supported by the Franz Brentano Foundation under the general editorship of Roderick M. Chisholm. I wish to express my thanks to the Foundation and its Directors, Professor Chisholm, the late J. C. M. Brentano, Sophie Brentano, Dr George Katkov and William Kneale for the opportunity to edit and translate this work.

Linda L. McAlister
San Diego State University,
Imperial Valley Campus
Calexico, California

INTRODUCTION TO THE 1929 EDITION

by Oskar Kraus

Brentano originally planned to follow up Book Two of his *Psychology From an Empirical Standpoint* with three other books, one dealing with the laws of presentation,[1] another with the theory of judgment, and the last one with the emotions and the theory of the will. He wanted to end this work with the mind-body problem, and a discussion of the question of the mental nature of the subject of consciousness and its fate after death. This was the draft sketched in the Foreword.

Although Brentano never carried out this plan, he continued throughout his life to investigate the individual topics mentioned and he dictated and wrote numerous essays on them.

There are a number of reasons why the plan in its original form could not have been carried out. First and foremost, Brentano did not take into consideration the distinction between sensory and non-sensory consciousness. Only non-sensory consciousness, however, exhibits presentations (Cartesian ideas) in their pure form, in so far as they occur with a certain degree of isolation in the conceptual act of presenting. The sensory realm, however, never gives us in isolation that which Brentano calls 'presentation'; what we as sensory beings experience are sensations (possibly phantasms and hallucinations) and affects, and in both instances the presentation is merely an integral basic component of the state of consciousness. After all, sensations are always instinctive, blind acts of believing in qualities, in connection with affects we not only have this belief, but also an act of loving or hating directed toward it.

Another reason why the original plan could not have been executed is the fact that Brentano did not draw the distinction between descriptive and genetic psychology until after the publication of *Psychology From an Empirical Standpoint*. Although this work deals mainly with descriptive (phenomenognostic) questions, Brentano would later have clearly distinguished between these and genetic problems in the structure of the work. The partially revised edition of 1911 contains only the descriptive question concerning the classification of mental phenomena.

I took this new edition of the Classification, together with its Appendices and four very important essays that had not been previously published, and compiled them in Volume II of the 1925 edition of the *Psychology*, while Volume I of this edition includes the earlier chapters on psychological method and the general doctrine of consciousness and the unity of the consciousness. Thus the present continuation of the *Psychology* (*Psychology* III, so to speak) which I have compiled for all those who are interested in psychology and scientific philosophy, and for which I have chosen the title *Sensory and Noetic Consciousness*, is simply carrying out Brentano's original plan.

Brentano regarded the classification of states of consciousness according to the differences of what he calls the 'intentional relation to the object', as the preferable classification. Analagous to his differentiation between presentations, judgments and emotions, he would have based the three following books on this tripartite division.

Even though it is true that the difference in what Brentano called 'intentional relation' is the most fundamental principle of classification, it is imperative that we take the Platonic-Aristotelian classification into consideration as well, namely the division into sensory and intellective states of consciousness. He says in Book Two, Chapter 5 of the *Psychology* that the latter cuts across the former.

I have already pointed out in my Introduction to Volume Two of the 1925 edition of the *Psychology* that after having characterized consciousness as mental reference to something and after having made the general classification into presentation, judgment and emotion (feeling and will), it is necessary to discuss the question of the distinction between sensory and non-sensory acts; only when we have done this can we proceed to expose the structure of sensory and then noetic acts, and finally we can show how the acts of *aisthesis* are bound up with those of *noesis*.

The division into sensory and noetic states occupies a prominent position in both parts of the present volume, but is emphasized in Part II.

'Inner perception,' Brentano pointed out, 'shows us mental states with sensory, sensible or with non-sensory, noetic objects.'

These two types of mental states are briefly discussed by Brentano, and thus we get a – rather sketchy – outline of phenomenal or phenomenological psychology, expressed from a different standpoint from that taken in the earlier books and in the original plan.

Everything that is referred to as 'phenomenological psychology' today was called phenomenal or descriptive psychology or psychnognosy by Brentano, and it differs from that branch of psychology that investigates causes, genetic psychology, as Brentano called it. This differentiation goes back to Brentano; its significance for the method of research in psychology and the humanities has been increasingly recognized since it was taken up by Dilthey.

The term 'phenomenological' psychology can also easily be traced back to Brentano's terminology *'Lehre von den psychischen Phänomenen'* and *'phänomenale Psychologie'*. But because Husserl, in his later writings, no longer uses the term 'phenomenological' as synonymous with 'descriptive-psychological', but uses it rather for his *'Wesensschau'* and 'Ideation', I prefer to combine the Brentanian terms 'phenomenal psychology' and 'psychognosis' and use the term phenomenognosy for both of them. Brentano's investigations have nothing in common with Platonic hypostasizations and fictions, with *'Ideaten'*, or with *'unzeitlichem Sein'*, etc. On the contrary, they are extremely critical of them and reject them.

Yet the word 'phenomenon' itself is ambiguous and it may well happen that anyone who uses it is called a 'phenomenalist'. However, the word is so well established and we have so often pointed out that we use it as a synonym for 'state of consciousness' that this does not prevent us from using it.

The term 'phenomenology' was used originally as a synonym for Brentano's 'descriptive psychology'. Today, however, it is supposed to denote the science of a 'world' discovered by Husserl – a science 'of whose enormous scope our contemporaries have not the slightest idea, which is a science of consciousness, but not psychology' (*Logos* I, 1910–11, p. 302). A 'realm which, like the science attributed to it, had to remain unknown' before Husserl appeared. The method employed to arrive at this new *'Wesensschauung'* is called 'bracketing', a method whereby the natural attitude is eliminated and replaced by 'pure consciousness'. 'This very method makes it clear', according to Husserl, 'why this region and the science attributed to it had to remain unknown. It is simply so that in the natural attitude we can see only the natural world. As long as the possibility of the phenomenological attitude was not recognized, and as long as the method which brings about an original comprehension of the objects resulting therefrom was not crystallized, the phenomenological world had to remain unknown. Even more, it had to remain a world that could hardly be surmised!!'[2]

I do not want to go into detail concerning the characteristics of this method, which, like all types of mystical thinking, disregards natural means to knowledge and claims to reach into a super-natural region by means of a special '*Wesensanschauung*' (intuition of essences). I would rather attempt to identify the kernel of truth in these exuberant claims.

I have repeatedly pointed out that in earlier times the extent to which *a priori* cognitions are possible has often been greatly underestimated. In particular, people believed that psychology as a theory of consciousness depended solely on the inductive and experimental procedures of the natural sciences. Yet Brentano already shows in his empirical *Psychology* of 1874, in his *Origin of Our Knowledge of Right and Wrong* of 1889, and, particularly, in his lectures on questions concerning the theory of continuity, that we can arrive at universal *a priori*, i.e. negative-apodictic insights in the psychological, value-theoretical, and synechological fields. This was the basis upon which his students developed phenomenology (Husserl) and the Theory of Objects (Meinong). Yet some serious mistakes were made in this development, e.g., with regard to the absurd doctrine of '*so-sein ohne sein*' or of 'Objectives' and '*Ideaten*'. These and similar fictions are mainly the result of the fact that these thinkers, and with them the majority of present-day logicians and epistemologists, refused to see the simple truth that all our axioms have a negative apodictic character. No *a priori* cognition tells us anything about a state of being or of being X; all it tells us is that something *cannot* be or cannot be X. Thus two contradictory judgments that are both evident are impossible, or it is impossible that someone judges or values without presenting, or that someone justifiedly prefers an increase of pain in the world to a decrease, or that 2 + 2 does not equal 4, or that the sum of the angles of an Euclidian triangle is not equal to two right angles, etc.

It is well agreed and beyond doubt that nowhere in the empirical world do we find ideal, i.e. perfect, triangles or perfect circles, but only approximations to such forms, to which the geometrical theorems are applied in an approximate manner. Yet the geometrical theorems state their theses with ideal exactness and not in an approximate manner. If someone, a captive of the language, were to take the theorem that the triangle has two right angles in its grammatical meaning, i.e. as a positive statement, and if that person knows that there is no empirical triangle which exactly corresponds to this theorem, then he must search for 'the triangle' which has two right angles as the sum of its angles in a world of 'irreality'; he must substitute fiction for knowledge.

If we realize, however, that this theorem merely denies apodictically a triangle with more or less than two right angles, then there is much less temptation to assume an irreal entity as correlate to that thought. At least as far as I am concerned, I can say that I first realized the erroneousness of the assumption of unreal things, of ideal objects, etc., in connection with these 'eternal truths'. The universal applicability and absoluteness of the so-called 'objectivity' of knowledge is preserved *in toto* if we apodictically realize that no person can ever judge correctly who judges contrary to that knowledge. What more do we want? Even Plato could reconcile himself to the downfall of his eternal ideas if he were to realize that it is not the judging man as such, but only the insightfully judging man who can be 'the measure of all things – of those that exist that they exist, and of those that do not exist that they do not'.

If we fail to realize that all apodictic insights are of a negative-apodictic nature, if we take them for positive insights, then we are very tempted to invent 'ideal entities', and to say of the person who cannot see them that he is not one of the gifted ones.

The reason for the invention of Husserl's essences or ideal objects is the same as that which led to the development of the earlier doctrine of 'immanent objects'; as a matter of fact, Husserl's 'essence' is nothing but a resurrection of the existence of the 'intentional object'. It is certainly true that 'concepts' (conceptual acts of presentation of something), for example, the conceptual presentation of the note C or of the tetrahedron, must be distinguished in the thought process from the object of the presentation, i.e. from the note C or the tetrahedron. Yet it is madness to believe that, because I conceptually present the note C or the tetrahedron, I can ascribe to this note C or this tetrahedron a 'reality' even though not a 'real reality'. This would be just as erroneous as attributing not a real but an 'immanent existence' to the note C or the pyramid which I present. Indeed, this older error must be regarded as less of a chimera, because after all, the rather unclear notion of the immanence of consciousness came much closer to the truth than the invention of a consciousness-transcendent ideal world of essences, in which all geometrical forms, among them all numbers from 1 (or from 0?) neatly line up into infinity in order to be intuited by thinkers in their 'actuality', which is not a 'real but an ideal one'.

Linguistically and practically harmless – even useful – fictions were used as the basis of the development of an imaginary theoretical structure. ...

Furthermore, if we try to discover the meaning of that mysterious 'bracketing', of that displacement of empirical consciousness by a 'pure consciousness', i.e. the consciousness of the phenomenological attitude, we seem to come to the conclusion that the person who engages in phenomenological psychology must exclude the 'natural attitude' in so far as he must disregard his own individuality and individuality in general. But this task is extraordinarily easy to fulfil. Brentano's research shows (cp. in particular *Psychology From an Empirical Standpoint*, Introduction and Appendix) that our individuality is not at all contained in a perceivable manner in our states of consciousness. Only general things are given in our perceptions; the present work also deals with this topic. We do know, *a priori*, that we are individuals, but we have no intuition of the individualizing element. Our external intuition, sensation, too, shows us only objects which lack final individuation. This doctrine contains nothing new except that it seems completely superseded by Kant's authority, according to which all intuitions are individual and all concepts universal; in reality, however, we see nothing but the revival of an old Aristotelian doctrine (cp. Brentano, *Aristotles und seine Weltanschauung*, 1911).

Hence it follows that every phenomenological-phenomenognostic universal cognition states something apodictically negative about universal objects, of which we have an original universal intuition, i.e. presentation.[3]

The theorems that evident judgments cannot contradict one another, that two contradictory judgments cannot both be evident, that two qualities cannot possibly be seen at the same place, as well as countless other phenomenognostic theorems, are perfectly exact, like arithmetical knowledge, and can be applied with this exactitude.

Psychognosy even has an advantage over geometry, because ideal spheres, cubes, prisms, etc. are never actual; thus the theorems of geometry which relate to them can only be applied approximately. However, we do encounter theorems that can only be applied approximately in the field of phenomenognosy, too, e.g., the theorems concerning the intuition of colour qualities, for an ideal red, an ideal blue or yellow cannot be intuited any more than an ideal prism can be found in experience.

Some poeple might also want to contest the primacy of psychognosy on the grounds that, as already pointed out in *Psychology From an*

Empirical Standpoint, we cannot do without hypothesis formation. To make psychological differentiations we must make comparisons, and this cannot be done without memory. Memory judgments, however, can under no circumstances claim to be immediately certain.

Even if we grant all this, we still cannot reject the insight that if we are dealing here with uncertainty of the first degree, so to speak, an uncertainty of the second or of a higher degree must exist in the natural sciences, for certainty as to the existence of a physical external world can only be acquired through certainty concerning the states of consciousness through which the physical is transmitted to us.

Now some people will wonder and ask whether we really want to substitute an *a priori* psychology for a psychology from an empirical standpoint.

My answer is: No! Our standpoint was then and is now an empirical one because that which we might believe we know as *a priori* laws concerning facts of consciousness, must be empirically verified in order to count as certain. Perhaps a brief look at mathematics and physics will help to clarify what we have said: if, for example, a modern mathematician constructs a four-dimensional geometry, he employs concepts which his synthetic and free creative fantasy develops by means of negation and analogy. Here, the existence of these constructs plays no role. Everything follows deductively with *a priori* apodictic certainty. A construct of this kind, if it were to exist, could not be anything other than thus and so. But it is quite a different matter if a physicist claimed that a four-dimensional world of this particular kind actually existed and that, e.g., we live in such a world. Now the actual existence of that construct would have to be empirically proved, and this is only possible according to well-established inductive methods of research, through observation and experimentation.

Phenomenognostic psychology frequently employs synthetic concepts and concepts that are developed by analogy by means of creative fantasy. Yet the psychologist does not want these concepts to be regarded as mere 'free creations of the human mind', he believes that they can be applied to psychological reality. Thus, like the physicist in the above-cited example, he must prove their applicability. Only then can he be certain that the laws that are self-evident *a priori* in these concepts are also positive knowledge.

The following objection will be raised: empirical phenomenognostic psychology claims to be based on direct inner perception, and in this respect to have an advantage over the natural sciences, which deal exclusively with transcendent things: bodies, of whose existence we have no direct certainty.

I reply: this advantage actually exists. It is not possible to doubt that we have states of consciousness, even though we may consider the existence of the physical world an hypothesis. Even more, a large number of psychological concepts and cognitions originate in the most direct perception, e.g., the concepts of sensing, seeing, hearing, feeling, the affects of pleasure and pain, judgments, the acts of affirming and negating, of loving and hating, etc.

Not only pre-scientific psychology – which in ordinary language has done a great deal of preparatory work for scientific psychology – but also scientific psychology itself obtains its concepts, to a large extent, from perception and direct apperception. But mental research encounters serious difficulties in those cases where it is no longer possible to notice and differentiate directly.

This is true, for example, of the origin of our concepts of time. The experiences which produce these concepts have not yet been satisfactorily identified by scientists. Assuming that Brentano has hit upon the right answer with his 'temporal modi' in these investigations, it would still be difficult to say that he directly apperceived them. Rather, they are at first hypothetical constructs which are invented by means of analogy and negation, and then an attempt is made, with their help, to give an explicit account of those facts of consciousness which we call time-consciousness. The hypothesis must be tested and all its consequences must be proved before it can be regarded as certain.

This shows that the procedure which is usually and justifiably called analysis of consciousness cannot come about without a complicated synthesis of concepts. Once the above-mentioned activity of the 'analyst' directs attention towards this or that element of consciousness, then it may well happen that this element is actually apperceived.[4]

Obviously it may also happen that the concepts at which the psychologist arrives turn out to be pure fictions which exist only in his imagination. This is the case, for example, with 'states of affairs' (*'Sachverhalten'*), 'objectives' (*'Objectiven'*), 'dignitatives' (*'Dignitativen'*), 'value constructs' (*'Wertgebilden'*), 'states of value' (*'Wertverhalten'*), Husserl's 'essence' (*'Wesen'*), 'ideal objects' (*'ideale Gegenstande'*), 'ideations' (*'Ideaten'*), 'non-things' (*'Irrealien'*), 'being such-and-such without being' (*'Sosein ohne Sein'*) and all similar chimeras which are invented by psychologists and epistemologists, but which, however, are not proved. They do not give us the slightest insight into being, rather they are mere statements about non-being. They are mentioned in *Psychology From an Empirical Standpoint* as well as in the present volume. If, for example, Anton Marty – and I following him – believed that we could account for the act of knowledge only by comprehending the correspondence between the judgment and some state of affairs (Marty spoke of 'content'), we, too, fell victim to fictions just as most epistemologists have, the latest being Bertrand Russell.

In his critique of my work 'Brentano's Stellung zur Gegenstandstheorie und Phänomenologie' which I wrote as the introduction to *Psychology From an Empirical Standpoint*, Ernest Mally writes: 'It is a rather difficult task to convince someone that he has thoughts that differ completely from those he finds in himself.' His remark is correct, but he should have written, 'believes that he finds in himself'. It was a long time before I could rid myself of the idea that insights which we have of this or that 'impossibility' must somehow or other have irrealia ('eternal truths', 'states of affairs') as correlates. Along with Marty, and like Husserl, I believed that there are irreal states of affairs which are somehow comprehended along with insightful acts (cp. Marty's *Untersuchungen zur Grundlegung der allgemeinen Sprachtheorie*, Halle, 1908, p. 425). Thus it cannot be denied that people have such convictions, and they can be explained, as is shown in *Psychology From an Empirical Standpoint*, in part as misunderstandings of the metaphorical and synsemantic character of certain linguistic expressions such as 'eternal truth', 'necessity', 'impossibility', etc., and in part as problems of psychological analysis.

The advantages which phenomenognostic psychology has over the natural sciences can only be called into question in those cases where we encounter great obstacles in connection with noticing and differentiating. Yet this does not change the fact that not only the subject of the physical research object, but its mental experiences and states of consciousness as well, are immediately certain, even though their more detailed characteristics often pose far more difficult obstacles to distinction and analysis than are posed by any aspect of the nature of physical research.

Pre-scientific psychology has simply accumulated such a wealth of established knowledge that an increase of this knowledge through the individual sciences is inversely proportional to the amount of knowledge already accumulated.

Another advantage of psychognosy lies in the fact that its concepts, provided they have been properly formed, allow for an absolutely exact application to the facts of consciousness and for the extrapolation of absolutely precise laws, whereas this does not generally hold true of physical concepts and laws. Even in areas where we have previously believed that we have discovered exact laws, this has been increasingly called into question, and we operate merely with statistical regularities.

The above statements indicate that there is in fact a certain analogy between the position of phenomenognostic psychology *vis-à-vis* experimental psychology on the one hand, and so-called theoretical physics *vis-à-vis* experimental physics on the other – as Lindworsky points out in his theoretical psychology.

I have just pointed out a number of aspects in which psychognosy seems to have certain advantages over physics, yet I must emphasize in this connection that phenomenal psychology is and will always be at a disadvantage in the area of experimentation. Very little can be gained by means of experimentation for phenomenognostic psychology beyond the area of sensory psychology in the widest sense of the word. It is erroneous to believe that the interrogation of untrained test subjects will bring about any considerable progress with respect to higher neotic processes, the theory of concepts, conceptual knowledge, inferences, or with respect to the doctrine of time-consciousness, or of noetic acts of evaluation. ...

Is it still necessary to defend phenomenognostic psychology against the attacks of the Gestalt psychologists? Their exaggerated self-praise has been strongly rejected in various quarters recently. Gestalt theory starts from the doctrine of 'Gestalt qualities' which was developed by Ehrenfels, a student of Brentano's, who was influenced by something Mach said in 1890 (cp. Ehrenfels, *Das Primzahlengestz*, 1922, pp. 7 ff). He tried to show 'that the similarity between melodies and figures – with their invariably different tonal and local bases – cannot be reconciled with the conception of a tonal or spatial figure as nothing but the mere sum of tonal and local determinants' (ibid., p. 16). The question remains whether or not subsuming both spatial figures and melodies under a single broader concept 'Gestalt' will actually further our knowledge; one thing is certain, however, namely that Ehrenfels was simply attempting to enrich 'descriptive psychology' by assuming a new element, the 'Gestalt quality'. His followers, however, turned the term 'Gestalt' into a slogan which they tried to use to eradicate all previous psychology, and analytic-psychognostic psychology in particular.

According to them, before the Berlin school of Gestalt psychologists, psychology was atomistic; it broke all consciousness up into 'sums' and 'conjunctions', into 'mosaics' and 'bundles'. A few particularly aggressive proponents of this Gestalt unity doctrine went so far as to call analytic psychology 'destructive!!'[5]

Perhaps David Hume was advocating such a mosaic and bundle theory when he tried to eliminate the subject which underlies states of consciousness. But where else are we to find the 'usual, piece-meal, purely subtractive-abstractive psychological analysis' of which Wertheimer speaks?[6] Brentano's phenomenognosy, at any rate – which formed the basis of the theories of Stumpf, Marty, Husserl, Meinong, and Ehrenfels, and thus also for Gestalt theory – never presented consciousness as a sum or collective, and never tried to make it a mosaic.

The very relationship between states of consciousness and their subject is one of accident to substance, according to Brentano, and thus not a collective relationship of parts. He also maintains that the relationship between the primary and secondary consciousness is again a very special one and cannot be characterized as a 'sum of conjunctions' ('*Undsumme*'). The analysis of the categorical, apodictic, and evident judgments, of acts of valuation and preference also reveals complexities of a very special kind which have nothing whatsoever to do with a sum. In sensory psychology the analysis of the spatially qualified and of the qualified as such reveals once again a number of special relationships which have never been regarded as additive ones. So much for the claim that Gestalt theory was the first to replace 'purely subtractive-abstractive analysis' with genuine analysis.

Phenomenognostic psychology is only one area of research psychology. Brentano distinguished between this and another branch which he called genetic psychology, and he himself undertook a number of important investigations of a genetic nature (I draw your attention only to his work on genius, reprinted in *Grundzuge der Aesthetik*, in which he traces the laws of association back to one general law, and to his critique of Fechner in *Psychology From an Empirical Standpoint*). ...

Phenomenognostic psychology is independent of genetic psychology; it is, on the other hand, indispensable for an exact treatment of all other psychological problems. But that is not all; there is no discipline in the humanities or in philosophy which is not dependent on the findings of phenomenognostic psychology. Philosophy of language and universal grammar, aesthetics, logic and epistemology, value theory and ethics, jurisprudence and philosophy of economics – while not psychology themselves – are all impossible without the phenomenognosy of presenting, judging, and emotional activities, as well as the phenomenognosy of sensory and, above all, noetic consciousness. ...

Though Brentano published his *Untersuchungen zur Sinnespsychologie* in 1907, they were first conceived of many years earlier. On 2 May 1907, he wrote to Marty:

> At the same time, the shipment from the bookstore in Leipzig will be sent to you. Let us hope that the publication will serve a good purpose. I feel as though I'm publishing someone else's posthumous writings and adding a few notes to them. Because of my eyes[7] I could not check the work again. My voice speaks from out of the past. And still it brings a strange new message to this world. I hope that it will be confirmed and will stimulate further successful research.
>
> I would like to follow this with a second book of about the same length concerning questions of sensory psychology: the principle of classification and the number of the senses, sensation and affect, nativism and empiricism, proteraesthesis, simultaneous contrast, light induction, intensity, on my interpretation in comparison with the old doctrine of the ἐντελέχεια ἀτελής , simple actualization in contrast to alteration, phenomenal measurement and estimation, etc. These raise a host of interesting problems, and one could show just how many things can and must be tackled in a completely new way.

A number of these questions, indeed the majority of them, are dealt with or at least touched upon in this volume. ...

In Part I, I have included investigations concerning primary and secondary consciousness, inner and external perception (*Wahrnehmung*), perception (*Perzeption*) and apperception. Psychologists and epistemologists will find valuable supplements to, and expansions and improvements upon earlier doctrines about knowing, perceiving, noticing, comparing and psychological method in general. The theory of direct and indirect presenting (*modo recto* and *modo obliquo*) from *Psychology From an Empirical Standpoint*, which has been virtually ignored, is put forward again, along with the theory of time presentation which is discussed in detail in Part II and which is regarded as a special case of presenting *in modo obliquo*. Thus the time problem which already played a role in the *Psychology* is discussed in both parts of the present book, in one case in connection with the explanation of the oblique modes of presentation, and in the other case in connection with the question of universal presentations.

Never before in the history of philosophy and psychology has such progress been made on the time problem, i.e. on the question of the origin of our time concepts and axioms, as is made in the investigations presented here.

Brentano and Stumpf had a major share in the development of the psychological theory of the origin of spatial presentation, a theory which has since been expanded upon greatly but which has never departed from its basic course. The present work, too, attempts to push further along established paths. No progress can be made with regard to the theory of the origin of time presentations without the 'temporal modes', and here again it was Brentano's acute vision which brought them to our attention.

As for the composition of this volume, I took a number of essays, the most comprehensive one being on the sensory and noetic objects of inner perception, and compiled them in such a manner as to give the work an external unity, and I hope a certain inner unity as well. It is my aim to unite Brentano's doctrines in such a way as to present them in a definitive form. But because Brentano was an active thinker until his dying day, and his own sharpest critic, it is not surprising to find incongruities even in essays written within a short period of time. In a few places, which I have clearly indicated in the notes, I have changed the text so as to make viewpoints which he had given up agree with the definitive doctrine.

In those cases where I am convinced that Brentano's final view is not the better one I have given my reasons in the notes. The notes also indicate the original titles of the various essays and their dates, in so far as I could determine them.

Part I, Chapter 4 consists of various statements which I have taken from several different dictations and from shorthand notes of oral discussions. Here, too, the source of each paragraph is given. This chapter is thus a mosaic of statements on the same theme, made at different times. That it can be rounded out into a complete chapter is one more sign that I have here captured Brentano's true meaning.

As for the justification of this procedure, I reply on a letter of Brentano's to me dated 13 January 1916:

> You indicate the task you have set yourself with respect to the
> manuscripts I leave behind. I don't know to what extent I think such
> publication is desirable at all. In any case, it would be better to do
> something similar to what Etienne Dumont did with Bentham's
> manuscripts. Marty has sometimes even compared me to Bentham in
> my reluctance to do final editing and to publish. But for that reason

John Stuart Mill did not want to consider the things published after Bentham's death as of the same value as Dumont's writings. Providence, which is always wise, has done many things differently than we would have thought advisable. Aristotle's *Metaphysics* was not finished, and none of his works that have come down to us were finally edited and polished. In my case, external and other circumstances make it hard for me to work, and thus many good things that I could contribute to my fellow men must be lost. It would be a foolish overestimation of myself to believe that this is an irreplaceable loss.

We see from these lines that even a free editing of the manuscripts would have corresponded to Brentano's wishes. But I still do not consider it right to go that far. It is, of course, unnecessary to give reasons why it seemed a foregone conclusion that I would retain Brentano's own words and give explanations and clarifications in the notes. In any case, the manner in which I have attempted to proceed carries with it less danger of falsifying Brentano's doctrines.

I do not agree with the final passage of the above letter. When Brentano was pressured to publish, he used to say, 'God could make an Aristotle out of any rock'. But elsewhere he admitted that with respect to our practical efforts, only the best that can be achieved by us humans comes under consideration, not what can be achieved by God. The loss of that which Brentano has to offer the present would be an irreplaceable loss, because experience shows that philosophical talent of this quality is extremely rare indeed. It is much more common to find – in contrast to the humility of the closing words of the letter – those who encourage themselves and others to believe that they, for the first time, have laid the foundation for a scientific philosophy! The more believers these pretenders find, the more urgent is the duty to make the richness of Brentano's thought accessible, in as undistorted a form as possible, if not to the present then to a more appreciative future audience. This is a task which I set for myself from the moment that I, as a student, recognized the incomparable superiority of this mind over contemporary philosophy.

My purpose was all the more intensified the more clearly I saw how much of Brentano's unpublished work sailed under the flags of his students – distorted to the point of unrecognizability, to be sure – without Brentano's even finding it worth the effort to claim his misused property. ...[8]

Here I will stop. Edmund Husserl has written to me, 'Brentano is a great historical figure – which in no way means that he is finished and done with once and for all – so there should be a certain timeless quality about the edition of his works.'

As much as I agree with Husserl about Brentano's historical greatness, I must point out that Brentano lived until 1917 and he took positions – mostly critical ones – towards contemporary philosophy, without this doing any harm to his meaning for philosophy.

I am also reminded of a review of my edition of Brentano's *Psychology* in which this work was compared to a Gothic cathedral which might awaken devotion, but where the flux of life is frozen in stone – while contemporary psychology was compared to a lively meadow in which everything was green and blooming. But all kinds of weeds grow in this field. I don't see why I am condemned to sit by and watch while the green growth of this meadow turns into a jungle-like primeval forest and buries the cathedral beneath it. Just as I feel it is my duty to publish and explain, I also feel duty-bound to defend that which I clearly recognize as being destined to lead us, not just out of the present crisis in psychology, but out of that of philosophy as a whole.

PART ONE

PRIMARY AND SECONDARY CONSCIOUSNESS

(External and Inner Perception)

PERCEPTION AND APPERCEPTION

I

INNER PERCEPTION

(Secondary Consciousness in the Narrowest Sense)[1]

1 If we define a sceptic as a person who denies that we know or can know any truth at all, then we could say that he is involved in a contradiction, for he is taking it for granted that nothing can be taken for granted. The sceptic may reply that he does not admit that contradictions are necessarily false, and that he is not taking it for granted that nothing can be taken for granted; rather he is making absolutely no claims and denying absolutely nothing. Now if he claims nothing and denies nothing, he does not have to be refuted. As Aristotle pointed out, we could leave him sitting there like a bump on a log, and just not bother with him. Nevertheless, it is worthwhile to find out what makes someone become a radical sceptic. We usually regard something as certain only when we believe we have a proof of it: this proof, however, is based on presuppositions and these presuppositions can, in turn, only be established on the basis of other presuppositions.[2] But this cannot be continued *ad infinitum*; eventually we have to assume something which is unproved. These basic assumptions are not certified by proof, and have to be accepted as certain without proof, otherwise all proofs based upon them would be unfounded thanks to the uncertainty of the basic principles. But what gives us the right to declare these principles directly certain? Is it some natural urge to believe them? If so, then what is to prevent us from feeling an urge to regard something false as true? This is what happens when someone gets an *idée fixe* yet we regard such people as fools. It also happens in the case of people who are not necessarily fools, but, having heard something since childhood which sticks in their minds, they have an irresistable urge to believe it. This urge towards

3

immediate belief is strongest in the case of recent memory or sense perception which depicts red and blue, warm and cold as given in actuality. And yet the belief in the actual existence of warm and cold leads to conflicts, for example someone experiences the same water as cold when he puts a warm hand into it and as warm when he puts a cold hand into it. Again, people are often ready to swear to things that their memory seems to confirm with utmost clarity, only to be forced to admit later that it was incorrect. Thus even the strongest urge towards direct assumption offers no certainty, and so it seems to offer nothing at all, if we tried to use the fact that everyone else agrees as a criterion we would obviously be begging the question,[3] for who can prove that there are others with whom to agree? Certainly not those others whose existence and judgments first have to be established.

2   The above statements obviously contain an undeniable truth; that the mere urge to believe something directly, no matter how powerful it is, does not provide any guarantee of truth. There must be something else that characterizes judgments that are immediately certain. We call this 'evidence' (*Evidenz*). What it consists of can only be made clear by comparing examples in which evidence is present with other examples in which it is absent. After all, this method − which we must employ elsewhere, too − is the only way we have of making simple characteristics clear. Descartes' example of such a case is the knowledge we possess in our consciousness when we are conscious of thinking, seeing, hearing, wanting or feeling something. No matter how much I doubt, he says, I cannot doubt that I doubt. And he does not mean by this that I have an invincible urge to believe in my thinking, but that I perceive the fact of my thinking with complete certainty.[4] What stands out about this case as compared to a case of a blind urge to believe can be seen by likening the blind urge to a deeply rooted prejudice. No matter how powerful the urge to believe may be, something is missing, and what is missing is what we call *Evidenz*. The closer we scrutinize the case of a blind urge, the more unjustified the belief seems to be, while in the case of evidence, it is revealed to be fully justified.[5]

3   Immediately certain cognitions are so common that there isn't a single mentally active human being or animal which completely lacks this evident knowledge. For mental activity always includes the evident consciousness of that activity. On the other hand, in cases where the activity is complicated, we cannot always clearly distinguish between its various elements, and thus our knowledge of ourselves as mentally active beings is sometimes clearer and sometimes more confused. Yet

whether this knowledge is confused or clear, it is always equally evident.[6]

4 *Aside from our knowledge of ourselves as mentally active beings, we have no directly evident knowledge of facts.* We do not even have directly evident knowledge of our own past or future mental activity. What we do have is an instinctive, blind urge to rely upon memory as well as on so-called external perception. But we have already pointed out that this urge is not evident.[7]

5 Some people will say that this is incorrect, that we also have directly evident knowledge of colours, sounds, etc., as phenomena, and even though we do not know them as really existing, we know them as 'existing phenomenally'. We ourselves are not 'phenomenally existing colours' so the knowledge of a phenomenal colour as such is not an inner perception but an evident external perception. They do not even want to admit that memory is totally lacking in evidence: they assume in a rather peculiar manner that a greater or lesser degree of evidence can be attributed to memory. They call it 'conjectural evidence' (*Vermutungsevidenz*),[8] and it is supposed to confer a higher or a lesser degree of direct probability, sometimes to infinity, approaching complete certainty.

6 It is easy to show that all of this is in error. If we investigate what it means to say the colour is not known as actually existing, but as phenomenally existing, it becomes clear that in the final analysis I do not know that a colour exists, but that I have a presentation of the colour, that I see it. When I do this, it does not mean that the colour exists, because otherwise someone might suggest that something to which I have a different mental relation, for example, something impossible which I reject as impossible, exists because it occurs within me as something denied. Nothing is within me, in the strict sense of the words, but my denial of the impossible.[9] Hence it follows that we do not really recognize that which is known as the 'object', what we recognize is only the mentally active being[10] who has it as his object. The improper use of the little words 'to be' which led to a distinction between two kinds of existence, real[11] and phenomenal existence, has caused a great deal of confusion in philosophy. Kant went so far as to deny that we can have real knowledge, while he believed that we do have phenomenal knowledge. If we look back at what has been said so far, we will immediately see the absurdity of this statement, since the so-called phenomenal existence of something simply amounts to the fact that something real exists, which presents it, sees it, and is thus mentally

related to it. If the knowledge of some real existing thing is eliminated, then the knowledge of so-called phenomenal existence is also necessarily eliminated.[12]

7 The doctrine of immediate conjectural evidence for memory must also be rejected at once as unthinkable. According to this doctrine something is known immediately to be probable. Yet immediate knowledge of something as probable is ruled out because every cognition of probability is composed of several cognitions, resulting from the fact that we know, on the one hand, that one of several assumptions must necessarily be true, and, on the other hand, that there is not the slightest reason to prefer one to the other.[13]

8 It is certain that neither we nor any other being who grasps something with direct evidence as a fact can have anything but himself as the object of this knowledge. Although this knowledge is always merely factual and not necessary knowledge, still we must establish the relative impossibility of the mentally active being existing as such while the object of the activity is non-existent. This is the case in self-knowledge, but not in purely factual knowledge of other people.[14] There is, furthermore, no contradiction between the fact that somebody believes he or she has experienced something earlier, and the fact that he or she has not experienced it. Therefore, directly evident[15] memory is completely ruled out, not just for human beings but for any other kind of being or thinking processes that are not immediately necessary.

9 This point is of great importance and for this reason it will be good to clarify it somewhat and to strengthen it against objections. For the sake of clarification let me emphasize that it does not suffice for direct factual knowledge that that which is known *is* identical with the knower. We must also *know* that the knower and that which is known are identical. If someone judges that a judging being exists, there would be a contradiction if his judgment were false. Yet if he were unaware of the relation of identity between himself and that about which he is judging, then this contradiction would be virtually non-existent for him. This shows how Lichtenberg made things worse instead of better when he tried to improve upon Descartes' '*cogito ergo sum*', by saying that we have to restrict the meaning of this statement to 'it thinks' rather than 'I think'. That would mean, in the case of a judgment, that the relation of identity between the one who makes the judgment and the object of the judgment would remain unknown. If this were the case, direct evidence would be impossible.[16]

10 Attempts have been made to refute the restriction outlined above

by saying that not only is it a contradiction to say that something simultaneously exists and does not exist, but it is also a contradiction to say that someone judges with evidence that something exists which does not exist. Assuming, therefore, that someone judges with direct evidence that A, as a matter of fact, exists, there would be a contradiction whenever he himself is not this A, i.e. whenever A did not exist together with him as the person who knows A with evidence. So people accuse us of having committed a simple *petitio principii*. But this is not so. Let us illustrate this case with an example. If we assume that someone knew with direct evidence some distant object to which he had no relation, e.g. a stone lying in a street in Peking, and that a contradiction were to arise and be recognized as such if someone claimed that the stone does not exist, what would we say of a case in which the stone is removed? The one who removed the stone would not influence me, and so my mental behaviour would remain unchanged. I would, therefore, judge as before that the stone was still lying in the street. My judgment would have undergone no modification at all and would thus still be evident. If one were to say that this is false, then one would have to admit to the belief that the actual presence of the stone in the street in Peking caused my evident judgment as to its whereabouts, or, vice versa, was caused by my evident judgment. If this were the case, it would also be part of the evidence of my judgment that I knew about this causal relation. Even then, although nothing would prevent us from calling this evidence, we could no longer regard it as direct evidence.[17] Thus Descartes claimed, in contesting the evidence of so-called external perception, that we would have to say that the object of external perception, by its actual existence, creates a true image of itself within us, and that nothing else could produce this same image; this is something which, taking into consideration the assumption of the existence of an omnipotent God, cannot simply be claimed from the outset.

11   Another psychological error that has been revived and has found new support must be decisively rejected at this point. The true circumstances in inner self-perception have been misunderstood in so far as people have believed that inner perception is not included in the activity perceived, nor given with it, as Aristotle said, ἐν παρέργω.[18] People have maintained that in some instances it is entirely absent, and if it is present it does not occur simultaneously, but rather follows, just as the effect follows immediately upon the cause as closely as possible. In turn it can lead to a perception of itself as a secondary effect, etc. Such a doctrine eliminates the characteristic element that makes the

direct evidence of self-perception possible; it omits the identity between the one who perceives and the thing perceived as such. In the Middle Ages Thomas Aquinas, no less, fell into this error and unknowingly departed from the doctrine of his master, Aristotle.[19]

12 The fact that directly evident factual knowledge is limited to the knowing being itself and, in effect, is directed exclusively towards the knowing being as presently existing, does not mean that this knowledge is not composed of a number of cognitions.[20] Descartes meant a great variety of things by his *'cogito'*. I see, I hear, I doubt, I am convinced, I feel a desire, I feel pain, I crave, I detest, I want, I am angry, etc., were all supposed to be examples of a *cogito*. And all these can be attributed simultaneously to the being who has direct knowledge of himself and, therefore, they can all be grasped by him with direct evidence. We have already noted that this can happen with varying degrees of clarity; it is now necessary to explain more specifically of what these varying degrees of clarity consist. Wherever we find greater clarity we are dealing with a number of cognitions. We understand something on the basis of several of its characteristic determinations and we also know their interrelationship. In particular we distinguish between them, and this means that for every single determination, we know that it exists, and that it is not the others. Thus, what we have here is a multiplicity of positive judgments. And for every positive judgment there is a negative judgment; not a purely negative one, however, but a kind of denial in which the object of the denial is affirmed. In the multiple knowledge which we encounter here, one part appears to be conditional upon the other.[21]

13 When factual knowledge is combined with the knowledge of axioms we find the number of cognitions again increased and increased by those which appear to be conditional upon others, just as, in the case of greater clarity, a multiplicity of cognitions is given, some of which appear to be conditional upon the others. These are negative judgments that reject something as impossible. If I know that a determination is contained within another, *I also know that it is impossible for something that is characterized by the latter determination to lack the former.*[22] Obviously, this knowledge is conditional upon the knowledge that one of the two determinations is contained in the other.

14 In those cases where we have clearer knowledge of the factual and axiomatic knowledge (of something as impossible) we are dealing with an expanded form of knowing. The expansion is effected by the addition of conditional knowledge; it may also manifest itself in another

manner, which we call 'inferring'. The term is employed if, on the basis of a number of beliefs, we reach a new belief, the denial of which would not contradict any one of these individual beliefs, but all of them taken together. Since the conclusion is not contained in any one of the premises, it is clear that people who believe that it cannot actually be regarded as new knowledge, and consequently as an expansion of our knowledge, are wrong.[23] It is commonly said that such a conclusion is known indirectly.

15 A further distinction is made between inferences in which something is concluded as certain and those in which something is concluded as probable. The form of a regular die may lead me to say, for example, that I can conclude with probability that if I throw the die one hundred times, the 'one' will come up more than once. A close examination shows that the inference process follows the same pattern. It is virtually a mathematical process; yet the peculiarity lies in the fact that the conclusion at which I arrive expresses something that relates to a lingering doubt that I have. This condition of doubt is called conjecture and we speak of degrees of rational conjecture.[24]

16 Everything that we actually know is of this sort. Many people, however, make judgments which go far beyond what they know. They do this even with regard to that which they directly affirm to be factual, for example, when they are directly convinced of a past experience or when they believe in a spatial external world, which, in turn, leads them to believe in the existence of other persons like themselves. All of these beliefs seem logically unjustified; nevertheless, were they to prove partially or wholly true, the question would arise whether, with the means of knowledge at our disposal, we would ever be able rationally to verify them. This has been denied. It has been claimed that there is no way of establishing the existence of anything but ourselves. People have not usually gone so far as to say that our previous experiences are mere illusions; all they say is that all of history has taken place *within us*. But we could go one step further; since only the present 'I' is directly evident, we must reject as unjustified the belief both in our own past and in a continuous development.[25] We could even go so far as to regard this opinion as preferable to any other. Such theories are called solipsism; one represents the radical form, the other is less consistently worked out. Before we can make a judgment about solipsism, we will have to survey the entire realm of the factual – that which is immediately before us[26] – and then consider the most important axiomatic knowledge, in order to see what kind of conclusions can be built on such a foundation.

II

INNER PERCEPTION IN THE NARROWER AND BROADER SENSES AND THE POSSIBILITY OF BEING DECEIVED[1]

1   We have not only shown that, as a matter of fact, none of our evident perceptions relates to external things, but also that it is wholly impossible for there to be such a perception – both in our case and in the case of any other thinking being. This is because it would have to relate somehow to an object that is known to be an immediately necessary thing (*Reales*). From what has been said about *Evidenz* so far, it is clear that as long as we are dealing with evident judgments no external change can make a true one false – something that can easily happen in the case of true but merely factual judgments, as, for example, when I continue to believe that I own a house even after it has burned down. Therefore, when I affirm an object with evidence I must be conscious of the fact that there is a relatively if not an absolutely necessary connection between the object and me as an affirming being. This, however, would only be the case if I were certain that the object perceived was caused by my external perception or vice versa. But since neither of these is the case, Descartes had good reason to point out that if a real thing[2] which corresponds exactly to the perception had really caused this perception in me, then God's omnipotence could have achieved the same thing. Thus I would not only lack the consciousness of the relatively necessary connection, but I could immediately prove that it is non-existent in this case.

It is true that there are certain cases in which something caused by something else takes on the character of having been caused by that thing, so that here, in spite of its omnipotence, not even a divine cause can be substituted as a direct determinant. This is how it is when, for example, we draw a conclusion and we realize that thinking the conclusion is motivated by thinking the premises, or when we are conscious of deciding on the choice of a means for the sake of a certain end. Yet there never seems to be a case where we do not simultaneously comprehend, *in modo recto*, through evident perception that which appears to us *in modo obliquo* in the evident comprehension of the effect.[3] Thus we see that the conclusion also involves the act of thinking the premises, and that the choice of the means also involves the desire for the end, and that the knowledge of the causal connection between means and end constitutes part of our inner perception. It is certainly true of all our acts of thinking that their very nature is that of a *passio*[4] and we might even say that this is universally characteristic of them. Since this would also hold true, for example, for seeing or hearing, which do not seem to stem from the mental; we could say that here, because a cause appears it seems to be certain that an external thing can be a cause. Yet, since this cause is presented with such a lack of certainty we can surmise only that it is a thing, but not that it is this thing or that thing, and thus we cannot say that it is some external thing nor that the cause might not lie within ourselves. Even if this were the case, it still would not demonstrate that something external exists, and thus it becomes clear that the existence of an external thing cannot be said to be guaranteed by direct perception. We might, however, say that the consciousness that our sensation is continuously caused by something is one of the contributing factors to our general tendency to believe that sensations are caused by the objects sensed and that we consequently have certain knowledge of their existence, although careful deliberation will prove that this opinion is incorrect.[5]

2 The above-mentioned objection is related to another one concerning the dependence which is characteristic of a boundary line as it forms part of a continuum. When we perceive ourselves with evidence, we perceive ourselves only as existing in the present; yet for something to exist in the present it is necessary that something else exactly like it or only infinitesimally different from it has existed or will exist in a continuum of temporal modes in which the present mode forms a boundary line between past and future.[6] Thus it seems that evidence would have to extend beyond the perception of our present selves to prior or subsequent selves.

In this connection it should be noted that these additional things that are known are always related to the self, and to nothing else. Then, however, we must keep in mind that if this boundary line must be part of a continuum, we cannot name a specific continuum as a prerequisite for the existence of the boundary line, for every specific continuum has a certain specific dimension. The existence of a boundary line, however, does not require a continuum of any specific dimension. No matter how small we can conceive it to be, half of that or half again, etc., *ad infinitum*, would suffice. Thus, with the exception of the boundary around which this discussion revolves, not a single additional point would be fixed as a matter of certain knowledge, no matter how near we may think it to be.

3   The proof that inner perception is limited to the present and does not relate in the slightest to the past or the future, even though we believe we have experienced many things and expect to experience others, makes it immediately clear that mental phenomena, like physical phenomena, can be presented and judged not just in a secondary but in a primary manner as well.[7] It is completely wrong to believe that when we think of a previous experience we experience it all over again with a lesser degree of intensity, as some people argue. When a person remembers a prior mistake, he does not make the mistake all over again, and when a person is repentant about an earlier moral lapse, he certainly is not thereby repeating it. The fact that I can have presentations, not only of my own mental experiences but also of other people's, proves that it is possible to have a mental phenomenon as a primary object, as well. Of course, the belief connected therewith, unlike inner perception, is no longer directly evident.[8] It seems that not enough attention has been paid to this fact, and this has contributed to the belief that inner perception is not always evident.[9]

4   There is yet another contributing factor. It has been noted that certain sensory deceptions, e.g. optical illusions, involve, in a rather conspicuous manner, a misjudgment of the relation between dimension and direction. With Zöllner's figures one gets the impression after crossing the parallels that what we intuit visually has changed considerably. In this case we say that we not only err with regard to the external world by believing that the position of the parallels has changed, but also with regard to the mental because we believe we have an intuition of lines which are directed differently.[10] We also say that affirmative judgments are negative and vice versa. And this has led to serious blunders in the construction of the rules of elementary logic.[11] We could list many other things which seem to indicate that we frequently fall victim to serious deceptions concerning what is given in direct inner perception and this happens in many different ways.

5   Yet we must be aware of the fact that there is quite a difference between someone falling victim to a deception concerning what is given in inner perception and someone not correctly perceiving what is given. Some people even make the mistake of believing that they perceive something through external perception which they actually perceive through inner perception. For example, many people do this even today when they believe that sensory pleasure and pain, like colours and sounds and warmth and cold, are to be regarded as sensory qualities. If that were so the qualities would be something given in external perception and their existence could not be known with evidence.[12] We also confuse a genuine sensory quality with pain when we say that pain is localized, e.g. a toothache is in the jaw, a migraine at one temple or the other.[13]

The deceptions that occur as a result of the trick with the ball that Aristotle describes and those concerning the elements which serve as points of reference in judging perspective, are particularly noteworthy examples. It is said that we have completely lost the ability to direct our attention toward these elements sufficiently to clarify their individual characteristics; this is because interest is directed exclusively towards actual things which, through their influence, cause our intuitions. Thus we habitually make judgments about external things without having any clear idea what our points of reference are.

There is a difference between perceiving something and noticing something, between comparing it to something else and then subsuming it under a general concept. There are times when such comparisons and subsumptions do not occur at all; at other times we make them but without being aware of how we do it. A variety of circumstances which occur in inner perception in a rather confused manner and without any clarifying analysis may be influential. Such ignorance can lead to all kinds of erroneous opinions. That which is perceived in inner perception often has a great many aspects, and not all of these aspects are individually and explicitly thought about and distinguished. If we have an intuition of a continuum we have an intuition of something infinitely divisible, but beyond a certain point we are no longer able to distinguish smaller components. Furthermore, equal additions are not always equally noticeable. The previously given dimension is essentially the standard; it is natural, however, to consider additions which appear to be equal as equal, and this is why Zöllner's figures and other no less remarkable cases are deceptive.

In making comparisons memory plays a role, and despite our natural confidence in it, it is not directly evident; this alone proves that we cannot claim the same infallibility for results acquired through comparisons as we can claim for those acquired through inner perception.

We mentioned above the error that some people make by regarding pleasure and pain as sensory qualities that are localized in a certain way and thus belong to external perception. We can say, however, in contrast to other sensations such as those of sounds or colours, pleasure and pain are affects, i.e. in their case sensing is not just presented and affirmed secondarily, but becomes the object of an emotional relation as well. It is love or hatred of the appearance of certain qualities, not of the qualities themselves.[14] But they are both intermingled, and it is difficult to prove that we are dealing with an appearance of qualities and not just with an appearance of the affect directed towards the appearance of those qualities.

The possibility of confusion on this point is shown by the fact that some people believe that the pleasure and displeasure which others feel in connection with auditory phenomena are given in the very act of sensing the sounds, this would mean that the sensing itself becomes the affect,* while always accompanied by a quality of a different kind to which the affect actually relates.[15] But we tend to ignore this latter quality and its localization in the same way that we tend to ignore points of reference in the judgments of perspective we spoke about above. The pleasure created by a musical triad cannot possibly be produced by the three individual sensations, for the triad is a unity and requires a special sensation in addition. We sense the same note when it occurs in a different succession of notes, but this sensation may be accompanied by pleasure in one instance or by displeasure in another instance. An unmusical person's hearing is the same, but he does not experience the same pleasure or displeasure.[16]

6   The reason that there are such striking differences of opinion among psychologists in descriptive psychology despite the evident nature of inner perception, is that so many kinds of confusions are possible in the realm of the mental. There is, for example, ample room for confusion about the question of whether we just have particular presentations or general ones as well; and about the following kinds of

---

*Translators' note: The German reads as follows '... in dem Empfinden der Töne selbst gegeben glauben, so das *diese* selbst zum Affekt *wurde* ...' There appears to be a grammatical error in the German here, making it unclear to what 'diese ... wurde' refers. We assume that, though feminine, it refers to the neuter noun 'Empfiden'.

questions as well: how many kinds of sensations exist; whether all mental activity relates to an object; if the relationship is a varied one, how varied is it; what kind of difference are we actually referring to when we speak of something present, past or future; what do we understand by the intensity of a sensory phenomenon; is any mental activity without a certain intensity conceivable; are the intensities of different kinds of sensations intensities in the same or in an analogous sense; every time one senses something does one localize the quality and does that which appears spatially in the sensation appear spatially in the same or in an analogous sense, in different kinds of sensations; does it appear extended in two or three dimensions, and, indeed, can we talk of continuity at all in this case: does the presentation of a substance or, for that matter, the presentation of something acting or being acted upon, form part of some kind of intuition? If we say no to this last question it leads to the view that the concept was created by the composition of many characteristics which have to be identified individually.[17]

All this shows, as we correctly pointed out, that we will often be confronted with the task of clarifying certain concepts in connection with certain facts from which they have to be extracted.[18]

7   Thus it seems to be correct to say that we have established the following points regarding direct factual affirmative judgments:[19]

1   Some of our direct factual affirmations are evident while others are the result of a blind urge.[20] We may call the latter instinctive. This blind urge is sometimes strong and sometimes weak; there are, however, no gradations of evidence.

2   All inner perceptions are evident. Yet one must be careful not to mistake something else for inner perception. If Zöllner's figures cause a person to make a false judgment, and if this person believes that his visual phenomena, as phenomena, have changed in a way in which they have not changed, then his judgment about that which he inwardly perceives is wrong, but it is not the inner perception which is in error. He measured[21] and was led to false judgments about the relative sizes of the angles. Yet he has clarified none of these things for himself, and thus it happens that he mistakes his judgment concerning the direction of the line, a judgment which, as such, he recognizes quite correctly, for something he believes to be included in the perception of the phenomenon itself.[22] Nor are our very frequent judgments of perspective a matter of seeing or the perception of seeing. We often feel insecure in such cases and venture only very

vague, hazy conclusions. It is also a mistake to think that we can have
direct inner perception of dispositions.[23] Furthermore, it is hardly even
necessary to point our that not all of our thoughts about ourselves are
inner perceptions. When someone wants to observe himself, he[24]
employs the intuition of a recent memory.

3   No so-called external perception is directly evident, but here again
we must be careful not to confuse those things which are matters of
inner perception with those which are truly matters of external
perception. A person would be involved in such a confusion if he
believed that the so-called 'phenomenal existence' of colours and
sounds were a matter of external perception. In fact, this so-called
phenomenal existence denotes nothing but the existence, as such, of
the person who is being appeared to, and this is something which
constitutes a part of inner perception. Recently some people have
wanted to classify pleasure and pain as sensory qualities. Because we
recognize the actual existence of pleasure and pain with direct
certainty, this would then constitute a case of directly evident external
perception.[25] Yet this is not the case, and if people say they perceive
pain or a pleasant feeling in a part of their body, they are perpetrating
a confusion which Descartes characterized very well. It is true that a
sensory quality appears, but the feeling of pleasure or displeasure is
not the sensory appearance; it is rather something that relates to the
appearing of same, i.e. to the act of sensation directed toward it, which
is a *passio*. The sensing is itself the object.

III

A MORE DETAILED DISCUSSION OF PERCEIVING, COMPARING AND DIFFERENTIATING
(An Essay on Descartes' 'clare ac distincte percipere'[1])

1   Descartes has given us two propositions which are supposed to serve as universal rules of knowledge. The proposition: '*quod valde clare et distincte percipio, verum est*',* and the proposition 'what is clearly and distinctly contained in the concept of a thing, can be affirmed of it with certainty'. Both propositions are somewhat less than perfectly clear. Descartes himself misunderstood the latter one, and as a result he developed his ontological argument.[2] We are dealing here with apodictically negative statements, and thus the proposition clearly is of the same type as the Law of Contradiction.

Descartes himself provided an example to aid in the explication of the first proposition, namely his '*cogito, ergo sum*'. He later said that in this example he had not meant to speak of an inference, but rather intended '*cogito*' to mean the same as '*sum*'. Otherwise one could assume that he had clearly and distinctly found a '*res*' included in the concept of the '*cogitans*', and, following his second proposition, had believed that he could affirm with certainty '*sum res*' of himself as '*cogitans*'. He erroneously regarded thinking as the substance of the thinker.

The proposition '*cogito*' is affirmative. Thus '*percipere*' seems to designate an affirmative judgment, but what about '*clare et distincte*'? In his work *De Principiis* Descartes explained these terms by using an intense pain as an example. The pain is very clear, but that does not mean that it is always distinct, for the person who feels the pain often

---

*This is perhaps a slight misquotation of *Meditations* III, end of section 2, where Descartes says, '*ac proinde jam videor pro regula generali posse statuere, illud omne esse verum quod valde clare et distincte percipio*'.

17

confounds it with his obscure judgment concerning the nature of the pain. This is because people commonly believe that there is something similar to the sensation of pain that exists in the afflicted part of the body, although the sensation is the only thing that can be clearly specified. We can say that Descartes is here touching upon the fact that people confuse the sensation of pain with an unpleasant phenomenon located in a bodily part.[3] But he could have expressed it better had he spoken of confusing the sensation of pain with a colour or sound sensation or some other analogous sensory quality, i.e. of confusing a mental and a physical phenomenon, rather than speaking of confusing an obscure 'judgment' with a sensation, since both of them are, after all, mental phenomena, neither of which seems to be located in any part of the body. ('Judgment' must be understood here in the sense of that which we assume when judging.) 'Clear', according to Descartes, is that which makes itself completely perceptible; 'distinct' is that which is perceptible in such a way as to exclude any confusion with anything differing from it.

Descartes says: Distinct perception is that which includes only that which is clear. Thus, in terms of his own example, he would be of the opinion that in perceiving pain people generally include their obscure judgment concerning the nature of pain in the perception of pain, and because this obscure part of perception is included, the perception itself cannot be called distinct. Thus a clear but not distinct perception would be one which is clear only in part. The clear part includes no unclear parts; but in addition to that clear part, perception encompasses other things in an unclear manner.

Descartes' way of defining the terms differs considerably from Leibniz's later definitions.

According to Descartes' example, the term '*percipio*' is used in such a way as to refer to cases of negative judgment, as well. He speaks of perception of 'eternal truths', for example that it is impossible for something to exist and not exist at the same time, and that nothing comes from nothing. They exist only in the mind.[4] Perhaps there is a positive mode of perception here in so far as we perceive that we know these truths to be eternal. Yet we are actually dealing here with a double knowledge, first the knowledge of the eternal truths and second the knowledge that we know them, which is something purely factual and temporal and would have to be connected with the perception of '*rebus*' and '*modis*' which is contrasted with that of the eternal truths. We encounter so many inaccuracies and obscurities we sometimes get the impression that when Descartes speaks of clear and distinct perception, he is thinking of a distinguishing characteristic of certain presentations – giving us the right to make a judgment – but not of a distinguishing characteristic of the judgment itself. Yet in this passage we hear him speak of an '*obscurum judicium*'. The application of the terms 'clear' and 'distinct' to our thinking of externally perceived bodies and to geometrical theorems makes it even more difficult to understand what he means.

It is interesting that he says of sensory perceptions that they seem 'to come from outside' (*ideae adventitiae*), while we create fictions ourselves. According to Descartes both perceptions and fictions seem to have the character of passive affections.

'Distinct' according to Descartes seems to indicate that any confusion with something else or any intervention of extraneous elements, e.g. any confusion of a part with a more comprehensive whole, is excluded. It seems to me that in Leibniz's version this is already included in '*clare*'.

If we ask whether Descartes considers both propositions to be axioms, we come up against his strange opinion that God has power even over the truth of axioms; but this actually destroys their whole axiomatic character.[5] We have already said that one of the two rules, when understood correctly, turns out to be a contradiction,[6] and so does the other one[7] if you understand it to mean, 'a judgment that is evident, is true'.[8] This may be a somewhat liberal interpretation, but it seems unavoidable if we apply the proposition to all those cases to which Descartes wanted to apply it. His 'distinct' then serves as an indication that, even in the case of evident judgments we sometimes err by confusing them with other judgments – that we are perplexed and are led to doubt and to make absurdly contradictory judgments. Hegel came to deny the Law of Contradiction and Epicurus contradicted the principles of logic and the theorems of mathematics on the basis of the weakest counter-arguments.

2   It seems obvious that the expression of '*clare*' is somehow related to *noticing* (*Bemerken*). It refers to something which attracts our attention[9] to such an extent that we notice it. In contrast, it seems that the expression '*distincte*' refers to a *differentiating*. It has to do with cases in which we not only notice something because it has attracted our attention, but in which we also extend our attention to something else, which we think of simultaneously; we compare the one with the other and differentiate them from one another. Experience shows that if we fail to do this, we very often come to believe that several things we think

of simultaneously, and perhaps notice as well, relate to one another in a way in which they do not. Thus, for example, we confuse phenomenal localization with that which we usually attribute to an external thing thought to be the cause of our sensory perception. In Descartes' example, the person who believes that the intense pain he feels is located in the afflicted part of his body has not succeeded in comparing a certain sensory quality which appears to him as a primary object localized in a certain way, with the emotional sensation directed towards it, in such a manner as to distinguish the primary from the secondary object. As a result, he attributes the localization of the primary object to the emotional sensation itself. This error has even further implications. For the phenomenal localization of the primary object is confused with a location usually attributed to the emotional sensation itself; we think we perceive a pain in our foot as having a different location depending on whether the foot is extended or pulled toward us with the knee bent, even though the phenomenal localization of the primary object remains completely unchanged.[10] Thus serious deception occurs concerning objects of inner perception, while obviously inner perception itself, as far as it extends, contains no deception.[11] But we may also arrive at the deceptive judgment that inner perception has revealed something to us which it has not in fact revealed, and if we know this to be a deception, then this may lead us to lose confidence in the non-deceptive evidence of inner perception.

3   In this context the question arises whether noticing and also distinguishing between things compared are acts of perceiving and whether these acts of noticing and distinguishing are in any way evident. With regard to distinguishing, we would then have to go on to ask whether it has degrees of perfection, and whether, for example, it is easier to distinguish between the tonic and the third, than between the tonic and an interval that is closer to it on the scale than the minor second; or whether it is easier to distinguish between the tonic and the minor second in the middle range than it is in the deepest bass range. If we say yes, then we have to ask what that means. Is it simply a higher degree of attentiveness[12] that is required in order to recognize the difference, or is it that it is easier to be deceived concerning the difference, to err about our knowledge? Or does it mean a lesser degree of knowledge, in the same way, for example, that some of the most eminent thinkers have quite frequently spoken of degrees of evidence, for example Pascal in his treatise on geometric method? But what else could one reasonably mean when one speaks of degrees of evidence[13]

20

except that something is probable to a greater or lesser degree? And direct knowledge cannot be a matter of probability.

In order to answer these questions, we must try to clarify the entire process that leads to differentiating between things. The person who differentiates compares, and the person who compares[14] notices the two things that he compares. He must direct his thought towards these two things in particular. What I mean is this: the object of an act of sensing very often encompasses a great diversity. The act of sensing relates to a whole in its totality, but, of course, refers to the parts as well, yet only in so far as they are given implicitly with the object; it does not explicitly stand in a particular relation to each individual part. There are, in fact, certain parts of the whole, for example those which are not large enough, which can never be an object towards which a sensation relates in a particular and, so to speak, explicit manner. If that is impossible, then comparison and therefore also correct differentiation is utterly impossible. So we already know that we can speak of things being more or less easily distinguishable, when in certain cases it is easier or more difficult to relate in a specific way to a part of the whole and to notice it as an individual part. Now comes the second task: to compare the things that we have noticed.* How do we do this? It is well known that if we want to compare two things from a certain point of view we try to keep this point of view as clearly in mind as possible. If we want to compare the length of two straight lines we superimpose one upon the other, if we can, thereby eliminating the difference that even lines of the same length may appear to have as a result of their location. If we cannot do this and have to rely merely on our visual estimate, we will look very attentively

---

*The question has been raised how we are able to determine temporal lengths as successfully as we are able to determine spatial ones in relation to one another. Spatial lengths can be superimposed on one another, and on the basis of such direct measurements we can also arrive at indirect ones. But temporal spans cannot be superimposed on one another and thus there is no possibility of direct measurement. Mach even refused to use the term 'equal', 'longer' or 'shorter' with regard to successive time spans, but would only apply them to events taking place simultaneously. This may be connected with the fact that he failed to recognize that everything which is at any given time present seems temporally to be wholly undifferentiated when it is present. In memory, however, events with the same temporal modes of the present and the recent past appear *in obliquo*, in so far as a previous act of perceiving directed toward them appears as primary object to the person remembering.[15] Hence it follows that the two times which I compare with one another are present in my thinking in the same temporal modes. I think of them as simultaneous occurrences, i.e. as an analogue to superimposed lines, because the latter are presented in the same spatial determinations while the former are presented in the same temporal modes. Therefore, it is only the inaccuracy of memory and not a difference in temporal localization – which occurs even in the most faithful recollection (and it is in just these cases that it is most apparent) – which impairs the facility and certainty of the comparison.[16]

at the one and at the other from the same distance, letting them impress themselves on the same area of our field of vision. While the first impression is still freshly imprinted on our memory, we superimpose it, so to speak, on the impression from the new sensation. For the fact that it is impossible to have two impressions in the same place in our field of vision simultaneously does not exclude the possibility of our remembering another impression from a previous sensation, nor does it exclude the possibility of our perceiving how we create such an impression simultaneously in imagination. This would facilitate our comparisons in the same way as the method whereby the lines are superimposed in sensation, if it were not for the fact that memory continually diminishes in accuracy and is, from the outset, at a disadvantage as compared to sensation. Thus not only in those cases where there is a long interval between two measures of music, but also in those instances where one is played right after the other, our estimation of their relative duration will still be less certain than our estimation of the length of a song and its simultaneous accompaniment.

It is quite clear that we have here a higher and a lower degree of certainty as to a result arrived at on the basis of comparison. Furthermore, we see that in those cases where two sensations differ only slightly from one another, there is reason to fear that our memories' inaccuracy is enough to make us uncertain with regard to the question of whether the objects exhibit any difference at all. Again, we realize that this mistrust prevails to a certain extent initially though it decreases as the differences increase, and consequently requires us to exercise more caution and attention. Once a certain distance has been reached one can no longer speak of a further decrease in difficulty; we believe that all difficulties are completely eliminated. We believe, for example, that we can differentiate with certainty between pure yellow and pure red, between pure white and pure black. A similar situation arises in a number of other cases, e.g. if we compare a sound and a colour, or a statement that denies something with a statement that affirms the same thing, particularly if the same linguistic expressions are used.[17] In these cases our differentiating seems to leave nothing to be desired in the way of certainty.

If noticing proves difficult, the highest degree of concentration is required, and the attempt to divide this concentration between two objects is bound to lead to failure. If we compare two objects, therefore, we first direct our full attention towards the one object and then towards the other. This illustrates that such cautiousness carries with it certain unavoidable disadvantages, as we have just demonstrated with regard to memory. In certain cases, therefore, it is an inescapable fact that we can never attain anything but probability – a high degree of probability, to be sure. What could be called complete evidence is unattainable.

We hope then, that the above elaborations have sufficed to explain what is true and meaningful in the Cartesian '*quod clare et distincte percipio*' which seemed to lack clarity despite the example Descartes gave.

4   I also believe that I may say that there *really are cases where one can attribute evidence to a judgment which distinguishes between two objects* or, I might add, *which establishes certain other comparative relations between them*. But even then we cannot say that we know the difference or some other comparative relation between them with directly evident inner perception. It is not that inner perception does not show such relative things. It undoubtedly does because all objects which fall under inner perception *in recto* have an intentional relation to a primary object as well as to themselves as secondary objects. Another reason is that I know, in perceiving myself as someone who concludes or who prefers something from some motive or other, that I arrive at my belief in the conclusion through my belief in the premises, and that I arrive at my motivated preference through this or that presentation or through previously existing aims and judgments. Thus here too a causal relation enters the realm of inner perception. What we said about the exclusion of the relative determination of the object of inner perception referred only to *comparative-relative determinations*.[18] (Relationships of continuity are not completely excluded in so far as something continual is present in inner perception in more than one way. All we have to do here is think of the parallel multiplicity of seeing with regard to that which is seen by taking into consideration its extension in space and the temporal modes in which it appears.)[19]

5   The question remains whether the act of differentiating and other comparative judgments are, in general, or at least in those cases when they are made with complete evidence, apodictic or purely assertoric. It is undoubtedly true that they can never have an apodictic character. You will agree with me if you believe that the person who distinguishes A from B, i.e. who recognizes it as being something different, affirms A but only as contingently given and not as necessarily existing. Thus A is not necessarily different from B, even though we may consequently make the evident judgment *ex terminis* that it is impossible for A to be something without being differentiated from that which I think as B. We

cannot reply here that it is impossible for evident judgments to be false. If I have the line $\overline{A\ B\ C}$, in which I recognize $\overline{A\ B}$ as part of $\overline{A\ C}$, it would be impossible for $\overline{A\ B}$ not to be part of $\overline{A\ C}$, or not to be shorter than $\overline{A\ C}$. We encounter something similar with all evident judgments; although they may always be merely assertoric, the statement that, if they are correct the judgments that contradict them are false,[20] is an apodictic, *a priori* insight of the form of the Law of Contradiction.

IV

SUMMARY AND
SUPPLEMENTARY REMARKS ON
PERCEIVING AND NOTICING

(Perception and Apperception)[1]

---

1   According to what was said above, direct factual knowledge consists of confused perceptions, differentiations between logically[2] and contingently connected parts of one and the same thinking thing and perceptions of the whole connected with such differentiations. This kind of knowledge includes cognitions of relationships of agreement and difference between simultaneous acts of thinking with respect to their objects and modes – in relation to the objects, affirmative and negative particular judgments.[3]

2   We can say then that something is in a person's consciousness in two senses: (1) explicitly and distinctly, and (2) implicitly and indistinctly. A person who hears a chord and distinguishes every single note that it contains is conscious of the fact that he hears them. But a person who does not distinguish the various notes is only indistinctly conscious of them, since he hears them all together, and is conscious of hearing the whole, which includes hearing every individual note. His consciousness, however, does not distinguish every part of the whole, i.e. the hearing of each individual note which is contained therein.*[4]

3   The perception of a primary object is always bound up with the perception of the connected secondary object. The thinking of a primary

---

*In a certain way every observation is directed towards ourselves. The person who analyses a chord actually apperceives parts of himself as hearer. He finds that, in so far as he is the hearer of a chord, he is at the same time the hearer of the individual notes. The sound does not exist, and that which does not exist cannot be observed. But in contrast, I, as the hearer, can be observed in various respects, among others with respect to that particular difference which differentiates between the hearer of one note and the hearer of another.[6]

25

and secondary object is given in one and the same ultimately unitary act, and the two (i.e. the primary consciousness and the secondary consciousness) are completely inseparable from one another.[5]

4   We must differentiate the above example from the following case: I notice, I apperceive, the act of hearing and I notice (with evidence) this act of hearing as self-comprehending hearing. If I *apperceive* my sensing, then this apperception is a motivated judgment. It is not an act of knowing motivated by purely conceptual presentations, as is the case with an *a priori* act of knowing. Rather, it is an act of knowing motivated by the sensing itself: I see something green and apperceive my seeing something green. Thus I perceive with evidence that the act of seeing causes the apperception in me. This apperception, however, is motivated by the existence of the act of seeing, and not by the concept of seeing. (If I am motivated to love a means because it is a means towards a certain end, then this love is not motivated by a concept but by a judgment.)

For an act of apperception to be evident one of the following conditions must obtain: a) it must belong to one and the same act as that which is apperceived[7] or, b) it must be a correlate, or, c) the apperceiving act must be motivated by the apperceived act. The last alternative is the case with, for example, the apperception of sensations or other acts of consciousness. Because if we ask ourselves how a fact can be known with evidence by an act of knowing which is not itself identical with this fact, the answer is that it can when the act of knowledge is not merely caused by the fact, but cannot be caused by anything else. The act of knowledge must have the character of being caused by that fact.

The act of apperception is thus caused by the act of perception and at the same time has the character of being motivated by the act of perception. It is being motivated in just this way that makes the act of apperception evident.[8]

5   If a substance (a subject)[9] has an evident perception, it is always a so-called inner perception, in which the perceiving substance in general forms part of that which is perceived, but is not always explicitly contained therein. It can at the same time have a second evident perception which must also implicitly contain the subject, and it can have a third perception as well which encompasses the two perceptions just mentioned, and which is also evident. If one of the first two perceptions is eliminated, then the third which encompasses both is also eliminated: the other perception, however, can continue to exist by itself.

Here I spoke of the perception which encompasses the first two as a clear one, but it can also be confused, in the case where the two perceptions are no longer given as differentiated.[10]

Nothing prevents us from assuming that we have a consciousness of ourselves as hearing beings which includes neither a consciousness of ourselves as seeing beings, nor a consciousness of ourselves as beings who compare ourselves as seeing and hearing beings. Furthermore, nothing prevents us from assuming that we have the first kind of consciousness along with the other two, provided we do have these other two. But this first kind of consciousness is all that remains when the seeing being is eliminated. And sometimes we can also have the consciousness of ourselves as hearing beings along with that of ourselves as seeing beings, but without consciousness of ourselves as comparing beings, as when we continue to see and hear but cease to compare ourselves as hearing and seeing beings.[11]

6   Thus we understand an act of perception as directly evident knowledge that something in fact exists. This is the case, for example, if something that sees knows itself as such. It is also the case if something that sees and hears differentiates between itself as seeing and as hearing; also in cases where, seeing something for the second time, it compares itself, as seeing, with the object of memory, which is now a primary object and regards the one on a par with the other; this equating, however, does not include the existence of the primary object of memory.[12]

V

PERCEPTION *IN MODO RECTO, MODO OBLIQUO*, AND THE PERCEPTION OF TIME[1]

1   There is no question that in sensing we have two objects; one is called the external object, the other the inner object. Aristotle said of the latter that we sense it παρέργω [incidentally] and, as a result, the external object was called the primary and the inner one the secondary object. These terms are not meant to denote a temporal sequence. Later on, however, Locke's characterization of the inner object as that which is comprehended via reflection gave the impression that he did not think that the external and the inner sensory objects were part of one and the same act, but rather that they belonged to two different successive acts. This would undoubtedly be a grave error, but there is an even worse one namely the belief that the sensation of the external object often is, and remains, wholly isolated from the sensation of the inner object.[2]

2   The process which sensing involves could also be understood in a very different way. There are various modes of presentation, and, in particular, there is a difference between that which is presented *in recto* and that which is presented *in obliquo*. If, for example, I think of someone who loves, I think not only of the one who loves but also of something else which is loved by him, and I think of this second thing *in obliquo*. The same thing occurs with regard to sensing in so far as we sense ourselves as sensing beings;[3] for when we do this, we sense ourselves *in recto* and something else sensed by us *in obliquo*. One might now attempt to construe the situation in such a way that we, as sensing beings, are the only things that are sensed *in recto* while our external objects are sensed solely *in obliquo*.[4] Assuming this interpretation to be possible, we will soon discover that it has the advantage of being by far

28

the simpler one. In the affirmation of the inner object the external object is affirmed only as phenomenal[5] regardless of the fact that it may later on lead to the affirmation of the external object[6] as actually existing. There is no reason why an affirmation, perhaps even a presentation, *in obliquo*, must always be preceded by an affirmation and presentation[7] *in recto*, nor is there any reason why it should follow from the fact that an external cause acts upon us and thus leads us to sense something, that the first object which we present *in modo recto* must be something external to us.

3　If we carry this interpretation a little further, we will find that the external object of sensation, in addition to having a mode of presentation other than the *modus rectus*, can exhibit various other aspects in its modes of presentation; this is undeniable if, as is always the case, we think of an external object as being either at rest or in motion. In both cases we are dealing with temporal differences; when something is at rest, it appears, both before and after, to be in the same place, while when something is in motion, the location appears to be different before and after. What is the characteristic nature of these temporal differences? It is obvious that the objects are not given a certain absolute place in the course of events, but we are dealing with determinations relative to us as existing beings and as existing in the present. Thus if we think of something at rest or of something in motion, then in sensing one external object is thought of as existing simultaneously with us, another as having existed earlier, and a third as having existed even earlier. If we remain true to the idea that in sensing we are ourselves the only objects presented *in recto*, then we shall add at this point that we think of ourselves *in modo recto* in the *modus praesens*. Yet we think of ourselves as something which, in addition, thinks of other things *in modo obliquo*, whereby some of them are presented in the *modus praesens* while others, continually differing from one another, are thought of in a series of *modis praeteritis*.[8]

4　Like the presentation of rest or motion, the presentation of a succession of sounds can also serve as an illustration. The difference between a chord and a melodic sequence can easily be understood. If spatial phenomena follow rapidly one after the other, e.g. if a glowing coal is swung around in a circle, instead of seeing motion, we see a glowing circle. It would be a mistake to believe, however, that there is no continuum of temporal modes in this case. Instead of a glowing point we see a glowing circle because the major part of the retina is stimulated. But this does not change the fact that in the same way as the glowing point appeared to be in motion before, we now see the glowing circle as being at rest, where the state of rest involves a succession of temporal modes, just as the motion did before.

5   Yet it would be wrong to believe that the series of temporal modes with which something appears to us here is a very extended one and encompasses, for example, the whole of a piece of music or a speech we hear. It is true that everything which I heard earlier is important for what I hear now, but only because of *unconscious dispositions* which, in part, influence the affect accompanying the musical phenomena, and, in part, make it easy for the memory to recall what was previously heard or what was thought about when it was heard. In many respects it is just as if it were still intuitively in consciousness in an ever more distant past.[9]

6   There are two ways, however, in which this revival can occur. One possibility is that the earlier phenomenon itself returns, but in a somewhat weaker version; the other is that I *remember* having had it, in which case I myself, as the sensing being, assume the position of the external (primary) object, while I comprehend myself *in modo recto* with the evidence of inner perception as a person presently remembering me.

7   Many people have racked their brains over the question of how a fact of history or something which, I, because of a prophesy or scientific forecast, consider to be a future fact, differs from that which not only is not, but has not been and will not be. That which belongs to the past exists no more than that which has never been and that which never will be. The strangest hypotheses have been put forward, and some people have suggested adding a third mode of judgment to the modes of affirmation and negation so that we could treat something we deny in a manner somewhat similar to that in which we treat something we assert.[10] In this respect there should be no further difference in the mode of judgment with regard to something in the more immediate or more distant past or future. It is hardly necessary to point how inconvenient this theory would be. The above observations show how very easy it is to avoid this inconvenient solution.

8   I would like to remind the reader that there are modes of presentation which, because of the fact that the act of presenting is the basis for a judgment, modify the judgments based upon them.

Such differences in the modes of presentation appear in cases where something is thought of *in modo recto* and *in modo obliquo*. The person who thinks of someone who believes in the devil thinks of the devil *in modo obliquo*, and, if he is convinced that someone does believe in the devil, he affirms this person who believes *in modo recto*; he affirms the devil, however, only as something believed in by that person, and hence *in modo obliquo*.

We saw that our sensing, which is of an external object, also has to do with a presentation *in modo obliquo*. In addition, we saw that this *modus obliquus* is a manifold one in this connection, in so far as something is thought as being simultaneous with us while something else is thought as more or less earlier than us. We may now affirm it as something thought simultaneously or earlier, or we may be led to affirm it not simply as something that was thought of as earlier, but as something that actually was earlier. In both cases we have only affirmation *in modo obliquo* which is connected with an affirmation of ourselves *in modo recto*. I never affirm something as having existed yesterday without affirming myself as existing today, and the latter happens *in modo recto*, while the former is *in modo obliquo*. Then I affirm a thinking being as such *in modo recto*, and that which is thought, not in the primary sense but in a modified sense, namely, as something thought (and in this way even contradictions can be affirmed without absurdity). The same applies if I affirm that Christ was born more that 1900 years ago; I am affirming myself *in modo recto* as someone living more that 1900 years after this event, while affirming Christ's birth only *in modo obliquo*, and it does not matter one bit that it is on a par with the birth of a centaur.* *In modo recto*, it must be denied; but it can be affirmed, without in any way contradicting such a denial, *in modo obliquo*. We also see that the fact that something which lies in the more recent or more distant past or in the immediate or more distant future can only be affirmed *in modo obliquo*, does not mean that they are all judged in the same mode. If I think of something that is affirmed or denied by someone, in both cases I think of something *in modo obliquo*, but that does not mean that I think of them in the same *modus obliquus*.

9 Whenever we think of something *in modo obliquo*, we are dealing with a relation. But a significant difference appears here. In some cases, as, for example, where we are dealing with relations of equality and difference, the relation can be reversed, so that we can regard the terminus as the fundament and the fundament as the terminus. So both objects can be affirmed *in modo recto* as well as *in modo obliquo*. In other cases, as, for example, when we are dealing with the relation between the thinking being and that which is thought, this is not possible. The

---

*Translators' Note: The German text here reads: 'und es verschlägt dagegen nicht das geringste, daß sie so wenig ist als die Geburt eines Zentauren.'

thinking object can only be affirmed in the primary sense while that which is thought about is affirmed in the secondary sense. If we consider the relation of being spatially adjacent, we have a case of the first sort, but when we consider the relations expressed by 'earlier' and 'later' and, in particular, by 'having been' and 'going to be' then we have a case of the second sort. I am, in the primary sense, later than Christ's birth. But one should not say that the birth of Christ *is* earlier than I. One should say instead that it *was* earlier than I. It is easy to see what we would answer in cases where we say that Plato existed earlier than Cicero. Here we have two things *in obliquo*: the one has to do with Cicero and is connected to my existence *in recto*, the other has to do with Plato and introduces a complication similar to the one contained in the statement that we think of someone who thinks of an event. Only in those cases where I affirm something as simultaneous with myself is it possible to reverse the relation and make the terminus the fundament and the fundament the terminus.

10   We said that when we sense something we use quite a limited number of temporal modes of presentation. Nevertheless, they are sufficient to make it possible for us to transport ourselves into whatever past times we like. The smallest finite dimension, if added to itself as many times as you like, will ultimately exceed any finite dimension. With regard to the future, perhaps the immediate expectation constitutes a small beginning of a presentation of something future, which then grows into infinity by means of continued reiteration. By using the distance between something later and something earlier which is contained in the intuition of the past, one could also try to achieve a continuation and an expansion going beyond the present into the future, just as we do in the direction of the past.[11]

As we mentioned above, if an earlier experience occurs in memory, it appears to be like an external object, and, with regard to temporal modes, to be only in the present mode or in modes which are very near to it. This is a mistake, but, by using various points of orientation, this mistake is usually recognized and is corrected.[12] We can do this sometimes by using more exact and sometimes less exact indications of the temporal distance from the present; because of their approximate regularity we employ the revolutions of the earth on its axis, the orbiting of the moon around the earth and of the earth around the sun, and in other cases the pendulum swings of a clock or the running of sand or water, to serve as units of measurement. We do not want to go into the question of how we can acquire physical certainty of the approximate regularity of these events, but it is a problem which can be solved very easily.

11   Yet we must not overlook one fact, namely, that the sensing of ourselves as sensing beings is an *evident perception*, and, if this shows us as sensing an external object, we must actually sense an external object. Someone who senses an object, however, has it as object *in modo recto*. Thus, there can be no doubt that we *also* have an external object as object *in modo recto* which is given *in modo obliquo*, too, if we simultaneously sense ourselves as sensing. The only thing which is questionable is whether the external object, in so far as it is an object *in modo recto* is only presented or is also affirmed, and, in particular, whether the latter happens without exception, even, say, in those cases where it has been scientifically proved not to exist. Surely we cannot attribute evident affirmation to it. And so the old Aristotelian view[13] seems to be the only tenable one. Yet the one we are rejecting here is very popular these days. It is usually formulated as follows: external things are only sensed as existing phenomenally, which, in effect, means nothing but that they can only be sensed *in obliquo*, and this only happens in so far as we sense ourselves *in modo recto* as sensing beings. Since this is done with evidence people then have gone on to attribute evidence to external perception.[14] And to compound the confusion, some people, without being clearly aware of what they were saying, have claimed of us as sensing beings that we are perceived in inner perception as existing only phenomenally, in which case nothing at all would be presented *in modo recto*, everything *in modo obliquo*, which is absurd.[15] On this point we simply have to go back to Aristotle.[16]

12   Let us, therefore, investigate once more what is given in an act of sensing, in order to get an idea of differences such as past, present, and future.[17] For at the outset this is what is at issue, and not how we succeed in according something a position, especially the right position, by means of memory or inference with regard to the past, or by expectation with regard to the future. As concerns the latter accomplishment there is no doubt that a gradually acquired disposition plays an important role, in the same way as we develop visual judgment for the intuition of space. In this case spatial differences originally given in sensation itself constitute an indispensable prerequisite, the same must certainly apply to temporal differences.

When we hear someone speak or sing, several sounds appear to us *simultaneously*, which are sung one after the other. But how do they appear to us? Some have said that they appear to us simultaneously because we retain auditory images of what was spoken or sung earlier. This cannot possibly be the correct explanation. Such images appear to be just as present as the impression stemming directly from outside. Where they are given they combine with the subsequent impressions just as two simultaneous things combine with one another.

Thus we must say, rather, that the sensation caused in us initially is followed by another sensation, and the latter depicts, as belonging to the recent past, that which the former one depicted as present, and so on. We will call these successive sensations *proteraestheses*. In those cases where a sensation persists unchanged, it also causes such proteraestheses. Then we have the sensation of constant duration from an earlier to a later point, i.e. the impression of persistence, as, for example, in a note which is held for a long time.

It seems that the phenomenal time period which appears to us in this way always has the same length, just as, spatially, the field of vision always remains within the same limits. But what kind of a change occurs when an appearance which is given initially as present is sensed as past and as even more distant past?

One obvious possibility might be that we are confronted with a change in the object similar to that which occurs if a red point located at point A is gradually displaced and becomes a red point located at another place on the line A B. In the same way as the localized red is concrete and consists of two characteristics, one of place and one of quality, any sensed object would be concrete, in which, among other things, we find a real determination that is at one time present, at other times more or less past. As in the first case spatial distances were given, here temporal distances from the *present* and the *prepresent* (*Vorgegenwartigem*) would be given.

Yet such an idea proves immediately untenable. An object which changes its position in space still truly exists, regardless of this difference in location, and still falls under the same general concepts. The red point that has been shifted is stlll red. But if something that was present becomes past then it no longer exists, and a past red point can no longer be subsumed under the concept of red.[18] A past king, as such, is no more a king than a beggar is, for he may have become a beggar himself. The addition of the words 'has been' is not augmentative but modifying; these words, like the addition of the adjectives 'thought-of' 'painted' and 'alleged' to 'king', change the original sense of the concept and replace it by something else.

This consideration might lead us to think that proteraethesis depicts a

34

very different type of object from that depicted by directly aroused external sensation; one might even go so far as to say that its object is no longer a real thing but something that is removed from all reality. If the entire real world were to be destroyed, it would continue no less to exist (*bestehen*)* as a past world, in a manner similar to that in which the absence of a real world would exist.

Yet this idea, too, seems utterly untenable.

Above all, proteraesthesis presents us with a continuous series which has as its end point the aesthesis of what is present. Thus the object of aesthesis would have to change continuously into the objects of more recent or more distant proteraestheses, but continuity is incompatible with heterogeneity. Since heterogeneity would be given between the object of aesthesis and the object of each proteraesthesis, the required continuous transition from object to object would not exist.[19]

Furthermore, it seems that nothing other than a thing (*Reales*) could be the object of a presentation. It is true that we said we have a presentation of a thought-of king and we know that he was something other than an actual one, but, in truth, all we really have is a presentation of someone who thinks of a king. By affirming the thinking being we affirm the thought-of king, etc., and someone who thinks of a king is something real as such. We say that we think of something not-round: what happens is that in judging we deny a certain thing is round, and think of something as identical with this thing.

Let us assume that we, in fact, think not only of things, but also of non-things (*nicht bloß Reales, sondern auch Nichtreales*): they could only be some kind of correlate of the things, for example the 'thought-of king' would be a correlate of 'someone who thinks of a king'. Thus a non-thing could never be thought of without thinking, at the same time, of a thing; it could never be, without there being a thing at the same time. This seems, however, not to be true in the case of a 'past sound'. It is not at all the same as 'a past thought-of sound'. It appears exactly in the same way as the one which I experience as present.[20]

If we now have an object in proteraesthesis which is just as real as in aesthesis, and one which corresponds in kind to the one we have in aesthesis, then it is not difficult to recognize that it also agrees with it in every specific determination. A tone, for example, which has become an object of proteraesthesis appears not only as a tone but as a tone of the same pitch, and, I daresay, of the same intensity. Otherwise an aesthesis

---

*Translators' Note: 'bestehen' is the word often rendered in translations of the writings of Brentano's one-time student, Meinong, as 'to subsist'.

would not always be followed by a proteraesthesis, because the decreased intensity would be a consequence of the partial diminuation of the object of the aesthesis. Thus we can notice a decrescendo as well as a crescendo.

What then is the essential difference in the content of the proteraesthesis as compared to the aesthesis?

The way to the only possible answer is clearly indicated. Sensing is mental reference to an object.[21] Such relations may differ either because of a difference in objects, or because of a difference in the nature of the relation to the same object. So a judgment is different with respect to its content not only in those cases where it has a different object, but also in those cases where the relation to the same object differs, e.g. one judgment denies it while another affirms it.

Thus we can say that proteraesthesis indeed has the same object as aesthesis, but that it relates to it in a different way, and the manner of relating varies continually from the aesthesis to the most remote element of the proteraesthesis.

The question remains in which of the three classifications to look for these temporal differences – under presentation, judgment or emotion.

Grammatically speaking temporal modes are not signified by nouns, which we often consider to be the linguistic signs for things that are presented, but by verbs which serve, in particular, to complete the nouns with a predicate, i.e. they serve to express judgments. This suggests that the differences are to be understood as differences between various ways of judging. In his *System of Logic*, Mill, in fact, talks about temporal modes of the copula, depending on whether something is predicated as having been, being, or going to be. There is no doubt that someone who says 'A is', 'A has been', etc., makes judgments with completely different contents; he affirms A in some way in all three cases, but in essentially different ways. Yet isn't it obvious that in the same way as we affirm or negate A as present, past, or future, we can also *wish* it as present, past or future? Since this is not an act of judging, it seems to follow that the difference in these cases goes deeper – that it must be based on a difference in the act of presenting which underlies (*substituiert*) both the judgment and the emotional activity. And, indeed, it is possible to have a presentation of something as we wish it in the future or as we could judge it in the future.

Therefore we will have to regard the differences in sensation which are demonstrated by the first examples of temporal differences, primarily as differences in presentation.

The further we proceed with our investigation the more convinced we become that this is true.

Kant classified space and time as pure intuitions and as forms of our sensibility; and because he had a particular liking for arbitrarily assumed symmetry, after differentiating between external and inner sense, he put each of the above forms into one of these two categories. The form of space belonged exclusively to external perception, so the form of time was primarily reserved for inner sense. If this were actually the case, then every sensation that was temporally differentiated would doubtlessly be directed toward its object not only as presentation but also as affirmation. Inner sensation is evident perception. And this means that we have a judgment-relation to the object. So one might believe that only by means of this relation is something of temporal certainty possible in inner sensation. Yet we must judge the matter differently when we find that the preference which Kant gives to inner sense with regard to time is completely contradicted by the facts. Just as surely as notes appear to me in a melody or as colours appear to me when I watch a dance, they appear to me in temporal flux, in a *successive* order. There can be no doubt that, especially in external sensation, we encounter not only aesthesis but also proteraesthesis. Evident inner perception tells me only that I presently experience a note as present, another one as past, another one as further past, but it does not tell me that that note which I now experience* as past I experienced the shortest possible time-span

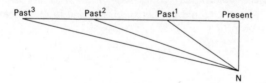

*The above figure illustrates proteraesthesis. The N at the bottom, from which the lines radiate, indicates that which appears inwardly with the temporal mode 'now'. All seeing, including the seeing as past, appears as present; other than that nothing appears inwardly. What was seen (*Das Gesehene*), however, is depicted in different past modes and the present mode by the line Past³ – Present above. If, in addition, a having seen (*ein Gesehenhaben*) were to appear, this, too, would get a definite temporal mode and would be directed toward something primary in different modes of the past. Furthermore, like a having seen, a having remembered the having seen (*ein sich an das Gesehenhaben sich Erinnerthaben*) would appear, etc., *ad infinitum*. We would arrive at an infinite number of dimensions. Experience does not confirm this in the slightest. We notice in inner sense, therefore, only the present point in time. This, however, seems, under certain circumstances, usually in fact – to be both the end and the starting point. At first glance this all seems to be highly paradoxical, and yet, on closer investigation, it seems to be possible, if not downright necessary.[22]

37

ago as present. This in no way has to be the case, as is confirmed by certain experiences of so-called double consciousness, where a person is stricken with an attack of apoplexy in mid-sentence, and only after a second attack that occurs a long time later does he continue the sentence; in such cases the first parts of the sentence, which were spoken months or even longer before, appear in proteraesthesis as though they had just been spoken. The evidence of inner perception is therefore, wholly limited to the present. This is true for inner sensation in general. It tells me only that I now have this aesthesis together with a continuous proteraesthesis of physical phenomena. If it were itself accompanied by an inner proteraesthesis as well, we could easily prove that this would lead to infinite complications, for its object would also have a proteraesthesis and so would the proteraesthesis, *ad infinitum*; this would result in a kind of continuum of an infinite number of dimensions.

So we see, in a certain sense, that just the opposite of what Kant claims regarding time has turned out to be the case. Particularly in relation to sensation of *external* sensory objects do we encounter temporal differences, indeed this is where we find most of them and a continuity of them. In another sense, though, but indeed only in a sense which Kant failed to make clear, it is true that everything that we perceive sensorily of temporal differences is perceived by inner sense and inner sense alone. For the differences that we perceive are not differences in the object, but, rather, differences in the way we sense external sensation, and this would not be comprehended in the absence of inner perception.[23]

PART TWO

PHENOMENOGNOSY OF
SENSORY AND NOETIC
CONSCIOUSNESS

I

A SURVEY OF SO-CALLED SENSORY AND NOETIC OBJECTS OF INNER PERCEPTION[1]

1   In spite of all restrictions that emerge from the foregoing considerations, there is an astounding profusion of things in the realm of the directly evident. A survey will require some general classifications, and, since many things that we differentiate prove to be complex in and of themselves, we must pay special attention to the elements[2] of which they are composed.

2   As we have already said, it is generally accepted that what we perceive with direct evidence is something mentally active;[3] Descartes called it 'a thinking being', in the broadest sense of the term. This expression, of course, can only be explained with reference to the examples given. What is characteristic of a thinking being is that it relates to something as an object: he who thinks, thinks something, he who sees, sees something, he who believes, believes something, he who loves, loves something,[4] etc. It thus happens that the thinking being, in thinking, always relates to more than one object; for example someone who sees, sees something coloured and at the same time perceives[5] himself as the one who sees. The relation to the coloured object is called the relation to the primary object, the relation to himself as the one who sees is called the relation to the secondary object; this does not mean, however, that they are primary or secondary in a temporal sense. The secondary object is always 'a thinking being' as such; the primary object can, however, as in the present example, be something which is non-mental. Nevertheless, it is also possible for a thinking being to be the primary object of our thinking, for example when I think back to an earlier experience or when I imagine what someone else

41

is thinking. Now, if every person who thinks relates, in thinking, to more than one thing – to one thing as primary object and to another as secondary object – we can differentiate between the person as doing the one or the other, and can characterize him in one or the other of the relations.

3   We just saw that the relation to primary and to secondary objects results in a certain multiplication of relations; such a multiplication also results from the fact that we often refer to the same object in a variety of ways, as, for example, when I not only think of an object but desire it as well. And it has been proved that such a duplication of relations to the same object also exists when we not only think of the object, but also believe it or deny it.[6] There have been psychologists who have maintained that the belief in an object, the affirmation of it, consists in a compounding of presentations. For example, in the judgment 'a tree exists', I would affirm the tree as subject and would add as predicate the presentation of something existing. This, however, is incorrect. For if it were correct, then someone who said 'an existing tree', would be combining the very same presentations, and would thus also be expressing a belief in the tree. Yet this is not the case.[7]

4   It is clear that all modes of relation to an object fall into three classes: presentation, judgment and emotion. The second and the third modes always presuppose the first, and in both we find a contrast, in that a judgment is either a belief or a denial, and an emotion is either a form of love or hate. We find a number of additional specifications within each class: we differentiate, for example, between assertoric and apodictic judgments. We speak of an apodictic judgment when we not only negate something, but deny it as impossible.[8] Furthermore, as mentioned above, we differentiate between blind and evident judgments, and between motivated and unmotivated judgments. I would also like to reiterate that there are certain composite judgments which cannot be broken down into several judgments separate from one another, since one judgment is, so to speak, based upon the other, and the second judgment, of which the first judgment forms a part, often unites a negative and a positive relation.[9]

In a similar way different modes of relation occur within the class of emotions. We find a parallel to the difference between blind and evident judgments in blind, instinctive love and hate as compared to love and hate that are experienced as being correct.[10] There is another analogy, namely, the distinction between assertoric and apodictic judgments. The analogy to the latter is exemplified by those cases where we prefer

42

knowledge to error, but where we do this in such a way that this preference is not only correct but is experienced as being necessarily correct.[11] There is also an analogue in love and hate to motivated and unmotivated judgments; after all, many things are loved for the sake of something else. The distinction between something which appears lovable in itself or only appears lovable in so far as it is useful, is a distinction that has no parallel in the realm of judgment; that which is established as true also appears to be true in itself, but it can in no way be 'more true' or 'less true'. We do speak of 'better' and 'less good', however; this is connected with the peculiar nature of certain acts of love as acts of preference.[12]

In the relation of presenting, we find no contrast similar to the one between love and hate or belief and denial. We can, of course, think of someone believing or denying something but in such cases, like those in which we think of something white or black, we are only dealing with contrasts that concern the *objects*. Yet there are other differences among the modes of presenting, for example presentation *in modo recto* and presentation *in modo obliquo*, or the differences in presentation involving continually differing temporal modes.[13] With regard to the first of these differences, let me repeat what I said earlier: if we think of a person who denies A, we also think of A in a certain manner; while we think of the person denying A *in modo recto*, we think of A *in modo obliquo*. And the situation is similar in all those cases in which we are dealing with something relative (*etwas Relatives*). A person who thinks, *in modo recto*, of someone who causes something, will necessarily think, *in modo obliquo*, of that which is caused, and vice versa. A person who thinks of something larger, *in recto*, thinks of something smaller, *in obliquo*, and vice versa. The differences in the temporal modes of presenting become apparent in the presentation of something at rest or in motion; if I think of something at rest, I think of one and the same object in continually changing temporal modes. When I think of something in motion I think of a continuity of qualitative differences,[14] but I do not think of all of them in the same mode of presentation, rather, I think of each one in a different temporal mode. Otherwise I would not be able to think of something as moving in a circle, because I would have, instead, a presentation of that thing occupying every point on the circular path. It has often been claimed that temporal determinations, like determinations of place, can be understood as differences in the objects, but this belief has led to hopeless absurdities. Caesar does not exist with the attribute 'having been two thousand years ago'; he does not exist at all. Rather, he existed – that is to say, when thought of in a certain past temporal mode he is to be affirmed.

5   We have just pointed out that the temporal modes are concerned with the mode of presentation. This, however, does not exclude their differentiating various modes of judging and emotional relations as well. On the contrary, this is universally and necessarily the case, because both judgmental and emotional relations presuppose an act of presentation. The relationship is similar to that towards objects: the same objects that are presented can also be judged negatively or affirmatively, and can be loved or hated. It is thus indeed differences concerning presentation which lead to differences in the other two basic classes of relations of consciousness. Among these, judgment often has a determining influence on emotional relations: love for an object is sometimes accompanied by the judgment that it exists, sometimes by the judgment that it does not exist, and sometimes by a conscious doubt as to whether it exists or not. This plays a role in the differentiating between joy and suffering, hope and fear, in the area of the emotions.[15] Likewise, the emotional relations that we experience are of importance for our judgments. We know that it is easy to believe what we want to believe, and if we cherish a love that is experienced as being correct, we know, as a result, that something is rightly loved and is good.[16] Yet this does not allow us to speak of a multiplication of modes of judgmental relation; rather, we are dealing here partly with differences in the objects and partly with differences in the causes. That is precisely the reason why judgment holds the second, and emotional relation the third place among the three basic classes of mental relations. It is also correct that a relation to a secondary object always involves a judgment in addition to the presentation, i.e. an evident affirmation,[17] while the emotional relation may or may not be present. After all, secondary consciousness is not always connected with pleasure or pain that would be given in the activity itself.[18] Thus the pleasure I feel when hearing a harmonious chord is not part of the act of hearing itself, if it were, it would have to have as many parts as the chord has and as many parts as we can differentiate when hearing the chord.[19]

6   Let us now turn to the differences which the mental activities that we perceive with inner perception exhibit with regard to their objects. They are divided into sensory and intelligible (noetic) differences. A person who sees, hears, or otherwise senses something has as primary object a sensory object and his secondary object, too, is regarded as a sensory object. A person who thinks of something *coloured*, *warm* or

spatial in general, however, has a noetic object, and his secondary object, too, counts as a noetic one. The presentations that have *sensory* objects have also been called intuitions; those that have noetic object have been called conceptual thinking, thinking of concepts. But people have not always been completely consistent in this, for they sometimes have also considered inner perception of noetic activity something whose object is an intuition.[20]

7   We are touching here upon topics where we have no consensus of opinion. There have been and there still are philosophers who deny the existence of the entire class of noetic objects. According to them all objects are sensory, and some go even further in their restriction of objects by not differentiating between primary and secondary sensory objects; for example they identify the coloured things that someone sees with his act of seeing.[21] The error becomes obvious if we note the fact that no mental relation is contained in the coloured thing. Furthermore, the contrast between belief and denial based on presentation may convince the person who is inclined to identify primary and secondary objects that this identification is quite impossible.[22]

However, we do not merely have a presentation of a triangle that is qualitatively and locally specified as well as determined with regard to size and form, we also have presentations of a triangle in general, a closed figure in general, etc. This will be clear to anyone who is aware of the fact that when we say, for example, 'the sum of the angles of a triangle is equal to the sum of two right angles', we do not think of huge numbers of possible triangles and prove the theorem for every single one of them; rather, we arrive at the knowledge of the general theorem in one stroke. Thus it cannot be disputed that there are presentations of such noetic objects.[23] The only thing that remains open to doubt is whether the intuition of a sensory object is always present when we think of a noetic object, as, for example, when a mathematician who states something to be true of triangles in general simultaneously has an intuitive presentation of a qualitatively and quantitatively specific triangle.

8   The objects of external sensory intuition fall into several groups,[24] i.e. we attribute them to different senses. There is no agreement, however, as to how many different senses there are; we usually distinguish five senses, but some have wanted to increase the number. Aristotle, for example, distinguished a sense of temperature from a sense of dryness and moistness. Some people have wanted to distinguish a special kinesthetic sense, others a special sense of balance connected with

processes in the ears, others speak of a sense of space and a sense of time. This shows that people have been unclear about what was to be classified, and that no adequate principle of classification has been established. We cannot speak of a special sense of space; every external intuition contains spatial elements given with concrete[25] qualitative determinations, and I can isolate the former by disregarding these determinations only by means of an act of noetic thought. If someone speaks of a sense of balance, however, then he isolates a special group of intuitions not on the basis of a characteristic that belongs to them as such, but because they provide a special point of reference for judging certain relations.

9   Aristotle established that all objects of sensory intuition appear extended and with a specific shape,[26] at rest or in motion, as one or as many, and so share in these determinations, and he established that although all of these objects are qualified from a sensory point of view, they are all qualified in a heterogeneous way with regard to each sense. Then he wanted to use the particular species of quality as the principle of classification, and he thus distinguished between a sense of colour and a sense of sound, etc. The idea was correct, yet it became clear that there was doubt as to whether certain sensory qualities are homogeneous or heterogeneous. Are the qualities of warmth and pressure and the quality of the sensation of being stuck with a needle homogeneous or heterogeneous? Some people thought they could extract an argument for the homogeneity of sensations of pressure and sensations of warmth by pointing out that if we approach a person's back with a burning light this light will give rise to a sensation of pressure. Others believed that the fact that certain parts of our skin are more sensitive to temperature, while others are more sensitive to touch, is an indication of the heterogeneous character of these sensations. Both arguments miss the point; if it is true that approaching a person's back with a light causes a sensation of pressure, while otherwise causing a sensation of heat, it is just as true that it brings about light sensations by stimulating the eyes, but we would not be tempted to call this sensation homogeneous with sensations of pressure and warmth. On the other hand, we would not deny that bitter and sweet are homogeneous just because the tip of the tongue is more sensitive to sweetness while the palate is more sensitive to bitterness.

Nor can the existence of different external organs decide the issue of heterogeneity. We know that if we were to connect the optic nerves to the nerves of some other sense organ, such as the ear, a stimulation of the eye would result in an auditory quality, while no appearance of colour whatsoever would occur. It should also be noted that we often attribute to the sense of taste that which actually belongs to the sense of smell; people whose nostrils are stopped up cannot taste the difference between an onion and an apple, and I myself have had the experience of candy tasting like eau de cologne, for nothing but the common sugary taste remains when the nostrils are stopped up.

10   We see, therefore, that if we use homogeneity or heterogeneity of qualities as a principle of classification and as a criterion to determine whether objects of sensory intuition belong to the same or to a different class, we need a further criterion in order to determine homogeneity. It was pointed out that a continuum might possibly serve this purpose; it is possible to proceed continuously from note to note and from colour to colour, but not from note to colour. But whether the former is actually true has not yet been proved with absolute certainty.[27]

Aristotle pointed out that there are two extremes in every one of the qualitative categories, e.g. black and white in colours, an extreme high and extreme low tone in sound. Indeed, it appears that there is not only an analogy to light and dark colours in high and low tones, but that a similar analogy to light and dark is found in all sensory areas. If we compare the impressions of cold and warmth and if we ask which of the two would be called light and which dark, the unanimous answer would be that the cold appears relatively light and the warm appears dark. The same is true of sweet and bitter, the sweet being called light while the bitter appears relatively dark. It seems that in connection with colours, sounds and temperatures, we are dealing with lightness and darkness not in the same but only in an analogous sense and thus we could say that we are dealing with different sensory areas when lightness and darkness appear not in the same but in an analogous sense.

Thus the question whether the sensation of temperature and other sensations of touch are homogeneous or heterogeneous resolves into the question of whether they can be said to be light or dark in the same sense or only in an analogous sense. Investigations have revealed that in this case they exist in the same sense. Certain deceptions concerning intensity of pressure are connected with this; if you move your hand around in a basin of warm water or of cold water, the latter seems to exhibit a much greater resistance, while in the former case the dark impression of warmth obscures the light sensation of the pressure. We can go even further and maintain that the lightness of sweet, sour, and salt tastes is homogeneous with the lightness of temperatures; this is connected with the fact that sugar water, when heated, is said to be less sweet. The same is true of smells. It not only very often happens that something pertaining to the area of smell is confounded and mixed-up with something pertaining to the area of taste, but that we speak of sharp and dull smells, even though the affected nerves are not olfactory, but tactile nerves. Another confirmation of the unity of the sensory areas for all these phenomena lies in the fact that the temperature of food, as well as its smoothness or roughness, seems to alter the taste, making something that usually tastes good taste bad, and vice versa. Another point would be the possibility that one impression is weakened to the extent that it is completely replaced by another impression, for example a spoonful of very hot soup conveys nothing but the impression of heat.[28]

Thus we arrive at the conclusion that sensory phenomena of primary objects fall into only three classes: colour, sound and a third class of phenomena that are qualified in a sensory manner.[29]

These are also the primary objects of those sensations which are sensory affects, i.e. where the relation to the secondary object is not merely a presenting and an evidently affirming one but an emotional one as well. Neither the sensations of sight nor the sensations of hearing are affects, even though they may be accompanied by affects; the same is true of some of the sensations of this third kind.[30]

11   Through the analysis of the primary objects of sensory intuition, noetic thinking reveals that the primary objects are not merely qualified and generically and specifically determined according to quality, but are also extended and have shape[31] and are spatially determined, both generically and specifically.[32]

They are also said to have degrees of intensity and this determination, like the one of light and dark, is brought into close connection with the determination as qualified; yet a number of things remain to be clarified.[33]

12   As concerns local determination, many people have believed that it does not occur in a homogeneous manner in each of the senses. Some have even gone so far as to deny that it occurs in any sense, as such; but if it should occur, it certainly would not occur in the sense of hearing. Those who have denied any local determination to sensory objects as such, have also, of course, denied that they are extended and have shape, since these both occur in connection with local determinations, that is to say they result from them. Those who adhere to this doctrine in general regard the connection of such determinations with the qualitative ones as an association based on experience. If they were asked, however,

where these associated elements originated, they could not give an adequate explanation. They are called empiricists, as opposed to nativists, and it is quite clear that the nativists are right. The illusory arguments raised against them amount to the contention that our sensory impressions are used to achieve clarity about relations in the external world, which are essentially different from the determinations that they contain in themselves. Among them are also local relations. Since these,[34] however, are not given in the sensory impressions themselves, but are acquired by means of experience, and since they are usually the only thing that is of interest to us, we generally pay attention only to them, and completely overlook the local determinations inherent in the sensory intuitions themselves. It is also a mistake to believe that local determinations are inherent to only one sense or to certain senses, but not to all kinds of sensory intuitions, particularly not to the sense of hearing. By comparing the impressions gained through the right and left ears we can easily establish the existence of localization. Other thinkers have doubted that different senses have a localization of the same kind.[35] They here maintained that various senses are localized only in an analogous way, this is completely wrong. To the person who regards taste, smell and the sense of touch as different senses, this fact will become particularly clear in those cases where their phenomena are intermingled. Yet this is only an *argumentum ad hominem* and does not simultaneously encompass localizations in the areas of colours and sounds. If, however, after closing his eyes and stopping up his ears, a person makes a sound, a local relation is established between the darkness in the eyes and the sound in the ears. This could not be done without the homogeneity of local determinations. Another illustration is the fact that something sweet seems not only lighter than something bitter, but also lighter than something warm, this is a distinct sign that we are dealing with lightness in the same sense of the word. Let us thus repeat: every sensory intuition partakes of local determinations and in a homogeneous sense.

13   Another dispute arose as to whether local determinations are only relative or whether they can also be absolute, and it is most interesting to note that many thinkers believe the former. Yet every relative determination also presupposes absolute determinations on which the relation is founded, if there are no numbers there can be no relations of numbers, and if there is no lightness, then there can be no relations of lightness, etc. In this context what would underlie local relations? Only qualities. But how can we find a local relation in some

49

qualitative difference, for example the difference between red and blue, or the difference between the notes C and G?[36] Just as we can be certain that there are local relations, we can also be certain that there are absolute local determinations, even though we often characterize them in relation to positions that we presuppose to be known, for example we relate all measures of length to the known size of the metre.[37]

14   Opinions also differ widely as to intensity; we speak of greater and lesser intensity. But we draw an essential distinction between the intensive and extensive magnitude; the latter enables us to distinguish parts, the former does not. When comparing two extensive magnitudes, the smaller is said to be equal to a part of the larger one, while we can distinguish in the larger one another part which makes up the difference in magnitude. In the case of intensive magnitude it is indeed true that one should surpass the other, yet the smaller is not equal to a part of the larger, because the latter is not supposed to be composed of parts. Why, then, do we say that one intensity is less than the other and not just different, distinguished, as we distinguish blue from red? Obviously, we do this because the difference in intensity signifies a greater or smaller distance from a kind of zero point. But what is this zero point? Is it a zero point of intensity and intensity alone, or does it mean that something else, in particular a quality, approaches the zero point, as when a note that was originally loud fades away? But there the quality is supposed to remain the same. How, then, are we to understand the alteration it undergoes, which brings it closer to the zero point? Is there a middle ground between existence and non-existence, and are there different degrees of the existence of the same thing? If a thing consists of parts, the destruction of the whole would be understandable if successive parts are eliminated; thus it is possible for an extended red gradually to vanish.

But intensity is not supposed to be composed of parts. The solution to this puzzle is as follows: Let us take the case where imperceivably small parts of two colours, e.g. red and blue, alternate in a given area − then the whole appears to be violet, i.e. as something reddish-blue. But it also appears as red and less intensive blue in an alternation of imperceivably small qualitative particles and gaps, and the single quality that is given here, appears to be less intensive. This means that here[38] too, we are dealing with an extensive magnitude, and a gradual elimination of extensive parts. It is important to note we are dealing with filled and empty parts of the sensory field, not with extensive parts of a space in the actual external world. We are confronted, so to speak, with a greater and lesser density of the appearance.[39]

15   From this it follows that all differences among sensory intuitions are derived, ultimately, from qualitative and local differences.

16   As to the qualitative aspect, we spoke of differences in lightness, which are heterogeneous in every sensory area, and which are not synonymous with each other, but merely analogous. In one and the same sensory area they are homogeneous, thus it can happen that two phenomena, even though they have specific qualitative differences, appear equally light. Doesn't that force us to distinguish between two other absolute components i.e. lightness and quality?[40] Some might still be inclined to assume that in certain cases there exists only one darkness or lightness that corresponds to the respective sensory area, while in certain other cases, the above-mentioned qualification is added. Thus a person might maintain that, as regards the sense of sight, black, white and the grey in-between are nothing but differences in lightness, while the so-called saturated colours reveal qualitative differences as well. Thus a red or a green could be of the same degree of lightness as a certain grey, but to the degree of lightness would be added another quality which the colour grey does not have. This would be a mistake in my opinion. Pure red has a certain lightness that belongs to this qualitative species, and this lightness would be the same as that of a particular shade of grey. But wouldn't that mean that the red is part of the grey in that it shares its lightness, since the grey consists of nothing but this lightness?[41] One would have to say that the grey is mixed in with it, i.e. imperceivably small particles of grey which constitute its whole lightness, alternate with other particles, that are red and which do not partake of lightness or darkness.[42] As to lightness, it would be the same as the grey, but less intensive, since the lightness would be less dense in it. If I mix grey with pure red, then according to this theory the infusion of lightness would merely intensify that already given. But this does not seem to correspond at all to the actual phenomena. In such a case we cannot speak of a greater intensity of lightness, but only of the occurrence of a deviation in quality, whereby the lightness remains the same.

17   What, then, do we understand by lightness and darkness? Should we say that we are dealing there with qualities which approach or recede from black and white? A closer examination shows that a red that is of the same lightness as a grey is further away both from black and from white than the grey in question, which, as opposed to red, lies, so to speak, on a straight line between the extremes.[43] Thus the simultaneous consideration of the distances of black and white would

lead to a disharmony of the determinations.[44] It is, therefore, advisable to retain just one of these colours, usually it is more practicable to use the distance from black as the determination of the lightness of a quality.

From this it is quite clear that it would be incorrect to regard lightness and quality as two separate special species of absolute determinations:[45] it is much more the case that lightness occurs inherently along with quality. Remaining are our two elementary differences – location and quality.[46]

18   Yet one could maintain that we would have to add a third element that refers to rest and motion, which Aristotle as well as modern thinkers, regarded as elements of sensory intuition and as differences in the objects of intuition. In this context I would like to call attention to what I said earlier concerning the temporal modes of presentation. If the temporal differences concern modes of presentation which then also modify the judgments and emotional states based thereon, it would be wrong to include these very temporal differences and the differences between rest and motion among the differences of the objects of our external intuition. Only in so far as we intuit something mental will we notice that it enters our consciousness either as a state of rest in the form of differing temporal modes relating to one and the same object, or as a state of faster or slower motion in the form of differing temporal modes relating to a continuous manifold of constantly differing objects. Kant seems to touch upon this point when he relates time first to inner sense.[47]

19   In connection with the localization of intuition another question has been raised, namely whether this localization is determined in three dimensions or only in two, namely length and width. The latter is often claimed, particularly with regard to the sense of sight. The fact that the visual phenomenon also includes points of orientation as to spatial depth does not contradict the statement that it contains no dimension of depth itself. We also speak of colour perspectives, and when both eyes act together the images do not always overlap precisely. The contours are blurred – sometimes we may even see two images – but they translate into a single line, and since it is this line which is of paramount interest to us it might be thought that this is what leads us to overlook the dualities which exist in the intuition. This blurring of contours was overlooked by earlier painters. It is also maintained, by Hering, for example, that visual intuitions, at least those produced by seeing with both eyes, are also extended as to depth. He says that if he looks into a dark corner the corner appears to be completely filled with darkness. A similar phenomenon occurs if someone covers his ears and makes a low rumbling noise: it appears as if the whole head is filled with this sound,

and the tingling sensation in the ear also seems to have a three-dimensional effect. The same is true of a headache, a toothache, or a hand being warmed; local impressions of touch are differentiated as to left and right, front and back, above and below.

In this connection it is of great importance to point out that to speak of something's being 'determined in relation to three dimensions' is quite different from its being 'extended in three dimensions'. Let us assume that the people are right who deny, with regard to the sense of sight, that it is possible to see through something to that which is behind it; even if we grant this, we could not go so far as to say that a determination[48] with regard to a third dimension is missing. The plane to which the visual intuition is limited would appear to have two sides, with the front one facing us.[49] If we compare a stretch of time with a line, it appears, like the line, to be extended in one dimension. Yet there is a difference, for the line is one-dimensional but has a local determination with regard to three dimensions, while this is quite impossible in the case of time. We may doubt from the very beginning whether it is even possible to have a presentation of something determined three-dimensionally which is not presented as being extended in three dimensions, and it is true that it cannot fail to belong to the realm of the three-dimensional. Yet that does not mean that there exists an extension of a determined magnitude in each of these dimensions. It is very important to make this difference clear, because a similar question will arise in connection with time, which exists only in terms of a point in time; the past existed, the future will exist, but only the present actually exists as the boundary between the non-existing past and the non-existing future.[50] And if we know ourselves with evidence in inner perception, then, as already pointed out, this evidence cannot go beyond the present and extend to certain parts of the past or the future. Some have wanted to conclude from this that the presentation of inner perception has no temporal mode;[51] as pointed out above, however, this is just as impossible as it would be to say that there exists a judgment without a mode of quality.

Returning to our question, the most probable answer seems to be that in certain kinds of sensory intuition there exists a spatial extension in three dimensions, but that there are others, in particular visual intuitions, which are extended in only two dimensions, but which have, in addition, a local determination[52] with regard to the third dimension. Thus the truth of our earlier statement remains unblemished – local determinations are homogeneous for all senses.

20   It might be asked how homogeneity of location with regard to all

sensory intuitions is compatible with the fact that we say in connection with one sense that the localization is a good one, and in connection with another sense that the localization is bad. That this is quite compatible with homogeneity is proved by the fact that localization in the same sensory area, e.g. seeing, exhibits great differences as to 'quality' with respect to different parts of the sensory field. It is wrong, however, to attribute the lower quality to the fact that one and the same stimulus leads simultaneously to different local determinations that mingle with those caused by another stimulus. In such a case, images could at least occur subjectively in the ear;[53] these, like those of the sense of sight would not only have extension but also shape. The true explanation is that shape and extension are based on the relative positions of the boundary points, and that they are known not simply by having a presentation of one or the other, but by means of a comparison. A comparison, however, requires special mental activities, and experience shows that special physiological requirements must be fulfilled in order for these activities to occur. In certain medical cases comparisons concerning local determinations are no longer possible, not even in those cases where they are otherwise very easy to make. This, therefore, constitutes the difference between so-called good and bad localizations, and not differences of degree with respect to certain specifications of [absolute][54] local determinations.

21   Another question comes to mind. We understood differences in intensity as differences in density; if a violet is as intense as a pure red, the red contained in the violet is less intense than the pure red, there are gaps in the red, which, however, are filled by blue. Now what about cases such as loud and soft? Here the gaps are not filled by a tone of a different quality. Shall we say that these gaps exist only with regard to quality? Or do they also exist for local determinations, so that between the qualitatively filled places, there exists nothing intuitive at all? Or should we say that only local determinations are given intuitively, because nothing but the quality is eliminated? We must say that there is no proof for the fact that intuitions of unqualified places exist. It seems improbable that a person who has never sensed a smell can sense the olfactory field, so to speak, and can present it intuitively. This seems to be just as wrong as the assumption that we have intuitions of a space that is infinite in every dimension, a space that, with the exception of certain small parts, is completely free of any quality.[55] (Aristotle ascribed intensity to quality, but not to location or local extension and shape, and even today intensity is generally closely associated with quality. This

seems to indicate that the assumption that the quality-free places are still given positively as local determinations, is the preferred one.[56])

22   According to what we have said concerning the difference between good and bad localization, the good sort is characterized by the fact that a multiplication of the thinking of local determinations occurs in which local determinations are thought of in relation to others. In connection with this newly-added thinking process,[57] as with all relative thinking processes, not only is something presented *in modo recto*, but something is also presented *in modo obliquo*. But neither that which is presented *in modo recto* nor that which is presented *in modo obliquo* is something so utterly new that it would not have been given as object in the confused presentation. Nor must we believe that we are thinking in abstract terms when we think of a part of the local extension contained in this presentation as something separate.[58] On the contrary, it is concrete and by no means free from sensory qualification with respect to its object. Animals, too, engage in this kind of referential thinking, otherwise they would not be able to differentiate between objects of differing shapes[59] and sizes; this, however, does not mean that they are able to present something in abstraction from sensory qualities. This very referential thinking which, when added, changes the otherwise bad and confused localization to good, clear localization is an act of sensing. One recognizes here, however, that the difference between the *modus rectus* and the *modus obliquus* of the act of presenting is already part of the area of sensation, just as the difference between the temporal modes definitely belongs in this area.

If one asks whether animals also comprehend differences in number when they differentiate between objects of different shapes and sizes, I believe that we have to agree that they do; and that we thus cannot be in total disagreement with Aristotle when he lists unity and number as common sensibles in his books on the soul. In opposition to that, it could be claimed on the basis of experience that no animal can count. Nor can it draw a picture of its master even though it can distinguish him from all other people. Although the animal can very well distinguish between people and animals, between horses and cats, it would not be able to give a definition as to the difference in species. Counting involves a peculiar, rational, methodical procedure, and someone might lack this ability. The particularity of the impression, however, which is caused in a sensory manner by an object that includes another one as a part *vis-à-vis* that part, can already be noticed in a relating act of sensing.[60]

23   Since we are speaking here only of those elements that show the

objects of external intuition, we note once again that due to the difference between confused and clear intuitions, we cannot speak of special object-elements that occur in the one or the other. Or is it more correct to say that in this kind of relating thought, something is presented within that which is presented *in modo recto*, and this something, as such, is not the object of a presentation of something absolute; for example the presentation of something bigger is not the same as the presentation of something big, even though it includes it. No matter how true this may be, I do not think we could say that when something is presented confusedly or clearly, the object of the confused presentation does not include everything that is contained in the object of the clear presentation. For all relations that are noticeable in the latter are already present in the confused presentation, but were not noticeable in the same manner as in the clear presentation. It is true, however, that the person who intuits something clearly, also intuits something which a person with an unclear intuition does not intuit. This, however, is something that belongs to inner intuition, since every clear act of presenting involves objects of intuition which do not exist at all in the case of a confused act of presenting.[61] After all, we do say that, for example, in the case of clear localization, new sensory activities are added.

24   We have differentiated the class of the objects of sensory intuition according to types of sensory qualities, and we have established three categories. Now we could go even further and investigate how many simple qualitative elements are given in each of the senses. In this case we could prove that there are only five in connection with the visual sense: black and white, red, blue and yellow.[62] Furthermore, we can say that in connection with the sense of hearing we have an analogue to black and an analogue to white, as well as a rather significant number of elements that act as analogues to the saturated colours. Those reappear in the octave mixed with tonal whiteness and tonal blackness and they occur in a relatively pure form in the middle octaves. In the third sense, too, the difference between dark and light also points to analogues of black and white, yet the analogue of black is even less pure than it was among phenomena of sound. Due to special difficulties psychology has not yet arrived at a satisfactory systematic classification of qualities. For our purposes, however, it is not necessary to dwell further on this question, just as we considered it unnecessary to deal in more detail with the question of special local determinations and the limitations of our sensory fields.[63]

25   When dividing mental activities into sensory and intellective

(noetic, intelligible) we said that inner perceptions of sensory activities themselves can be counted as sensory activities; thus we also have mental objects in the sensory realm, and these mental objects are not just secondary objects, but primary ones as well. The very same thing that appears as object of inner perception, also appears as object of an act of memory, and becomes a primary instead of a secondary object, just as if we had ascribed it to a mentally active being other than ourselves.

This fact has been misunderstood by many psychologists and even today we frequently encounter theories to the contrary stating that if we think back to something that we experienced earlier, all we do is experience in ourselves the earlier activities, though in a weaker form. These theorists have not realized the ridiculous consequences that result. A person who remembers an error that he made earlier and rejects it as error would be committing the error all over again. You would have to be careful not to repent your earlier sins, because you could not do this without committing them over again, at least in so far as the will was involved.

In the preceding discussion, when we spoke of the difference between confused and clear localization, we saw how mental activities which relate to something local and sensorily qualified become complicated when it is not merely a matter of comprehending, but when the local and sensory qualifications are related to each other. This relation, too, is part of the realm of the senses. It can become a secondary object and, consequently, a primary object.

26   After the discussion of non-mental sensory objects we must now discuss sensory objects, in so far as *they are mental*.[64] The variety is much greater here than among non-mental sensory objects. This is because every difference in the non-mental area corresponds to a difference in the mental area (if colour differs from sound, then seeing differs from hearing); and there are other differences as well. We have previously noted that we encounter the difference between presentation, judgment and emotion in the sensory area. We also pointed out that there are sometimes evident judgments in this realm.[65] The evident judgments, however, are contrasted with blind ones, e.g. reliance on memory, the belief in the external world, and, in my opinion, also, estimations of differences. It is easy to show that deceptions often occur here, and that in other cases the estimations are rather uncertain. If we take a closer look we will realize that complete certainty and exactness can never be achieved. These judgments simply assert that something is greater or less than something else, this seems to be incompatible with

evidence.[66] The fact that in the sensory area the difference between presentation *in modo recto* and *in modo obliquo* exists is shown by the fact that we attribute the character of a relation to this difference,[67] and to some of its objects. Every mental object as such is something which relates to an object,[68] and we have seen that new relations are added in the process of clarification. Just as there is a difference between *modus rectus* and *modus obliquus* there is also a difference in the temporal modes[69] of the act of presentation. Only in so far as this difference becomes noticeable, can we have a presentation of something at rest, or changing or in motion. A body appears to be at rest if we sensorily perceive that we sense it, in a continuity of temporal modes, at one and the same location. The question arises whether qualitative modes of judgment occur in the sensory realm, in so far as they have mental activities as objects; in more precise terms whether the negative quality occurs in addition to the affirmative quality. Since we already have the difference between evident and blind judgments in the sensory area, as well as the difference between simple and referential judgments, we might be tempted to attribute the difference between affirmation and negation to it as well. Yet not all psychologists do this – e.g. Nicholas of Cusa, to mention one famous name. In his *De Docta Ignorantia*, where he lists sense, mind and a third higher intellective power which we would call reason, he characterizes sense *vis-à-vis* the mind in such a way that sense always affirms, while the mind both affirms and negates; of his third, higher function he says that it only negates. Experience, however, does not seem to be in agreement with Nicholas of Cusa at all. Animals seem to experience not only love but also hate; they also seem not only to affirm but also to negate. If an animal which is afraid runs away, obviously it does not have a positive motivation to be somewhere else; but rather a negative motivation to remain where it is. And if a dog runs through all the rooms looking for his master, and, after having looked into one room, leaves it in order to look somewhere else, it is surely not wrong to assume that the dog made the judgment that his master was not in the room.[70] Generally, however, we attribute only sensory life to animals, and thus it seems that negative judgments are already present in the sensory realm. And if a confused presentation becomes a clear one, then one must recognize that an important role will be ascribed to negative judgments in the differentiation of the parts, where every part is recognized as something different.[71]

27   It is hardly necessary to point out that mental activities which themselves relate to something mental as primary object, can become

primary objects, just as other mental activities can, for example you can remember that you remembered. The major complications that arise in such cases pose no special problems.

28   The sensory emotions are also called affects; among them are pleasure and pain,[72] which have frequently been classified as sensory qualities rather than emotions, by maintaining that one feels pleasure and pain[73] in the same way that one sees colours or hears sounds. Yet it becomes immediately clear that this theory is utterly wrong, since the existence of pleasure and pain cannot be doubted like that of red or blue. Pleasure and pain are not sensory qualities, nor are they mental relations which would have sensory qualities as objects *in modo recto*; they relate to something mental as object: the sensation of certain sensory qualities is pleasant or unpleasant. This sensation itself is not a mere sensory presentation or affirmation, but also a sensory emotional relation and is directed towards itself as object. This has often led to another mistake. Some thinkers maintain that this sensation has no object at all; for example Sir William Hamilton[74] who said that, in connection with pleasure and pain, everything is subjectively subjective. He does not realize the inconsistency of his statement: he speaks of a subject and denies the object, whereas he overlooks that the subject is a subject only because of its relation to an object. Pleasure and pain, therefore, are genuine affects to which many others must be added, such as longing, feeling, hoping, fearing, anger, and the like.[75]

29   The sensory act of presenting, in so far as it relates to something mental, exhibits no location *in modo recto* but it does *in modo obliquo*.[76] The error arose from the fact that pleasure and pain were confused with the sensorily qualified, which appears localized, and to which pleasure and pain relate *in modo obliquo*. Thus people say, 'I have a headache on the left side and a pain in my foot'.[77] Yet the foot can be amputated and the pain is still perceived with evidence, but certainly not in the foot with evidence, since the foot no longer exists.

In this case, therefore, we cannot attribute continuity of place to the object; this, however, does not mean that it has no continuity at all. The act of seeing *per se* has no local parts either, but every part of the spatial extension which we see corresponds to some other part of the act of seeing. If the seeing, as such, must have continuity, this does not mean that it is continuous and multiple, but rather that it is merely continuous in a multiple way; after all we do not recognize many seeing beings in one seeing being, but rather a seeing being that sees many things. If the seeing being were composed of many seeing parts, one of which saw only the head and another only the legs, then there would be no being that would see the whole figure.[78] In a similar way we must say that if we have a sensory inner perception of ourselves as seeing and hearing beings and as remembering beings, and as beings moved by a variety of affects, we do not perceive many different things but one many-faceted thing.

30   If we recognize, however, that in this case we have only a single thing as object, then this also shows that we perceive that thing only in general, because we can, without contradiction, imagine that another being has the very same determination as the being that we perceive. Thus someone else could have the same visual presentations, the same sensory judgments and sensory affects. So these things do not constitute the individuality of that which we inwardly perceive.[79]

31   As concerns non-mental primary objects, the same holds true with regard to the spatial.[80]

32   There is yet another respect in which mental objects of sensory perception constitute a continuum! We said that we have presentations of non-mental primary objects with different temporal modes; thus something appears to us either at rest or in motion. The act of presenting allows us to differentiate a whole continuity of temporal modes, and thus itself appears as a continuum. But again we are dealing with a continuous manifold rather than a continuous multiplicity, and as such it appears one-dimensional, while with regard to local continuity of the primary object it has more dimensions. Either it appears, throughout, with three dimensions or, in cases where it should have only two dimensions, for example seeing, it appears in such a way that what we see in two dimensions clearly exhibits the character of something which belongs to the realm of the three-dimensional.[81]

33   Now the question arises, whether the mental object of our inner perception, which does not appear to us as something local but only as something relating to the local, likewise appears to us not as something temporal, but as relating to the temporal.

After what we have said concerning the temporal modes,[82] the question arises whether presentations, affirmations and possibly emotional relations, which we comprehend secondarily, are comprehended with *modis temporalibus*. We said above that the act of presentation requires a *modus temporalis* in the same way that a judgment requires a qualitative mode. Therefore, it seems that we must answer affirmatively. If we proceed however, to ask whether we have presentations of and perceive ourselves in inner perception in *one* or in *several* temporal modes, then the answer must be that we perceive ourselves in only one mode, the *modus praesens*. But then, since the present is nothing but a boundary line in a temporal continuum, the characteristic of belonging to a one-dimensional continuum is typical of the *modus praesens*, in the same way that the two-dimensional extention mentioned above has the character of belonging to the realm of the three-dimensional.[83]

One might believe it to be inconceivable that something two-dimensional could belong to the realm of the three-dimensional because if one comprehended that as belonging to the realm of the three-dimensional, one would have to have a presentation of something three-dimensional; and in the same way if one comprehended something without dimension as belonging to the realm of the one-dimensional, then the presentation of something one-dimensional would be indispensable. Yet in response we can say that forming part of a continuum, i.e. being a boundary in a continuum, does not require the presentation of any specifically extended continuum, for example as concerns space it does not require the presentation of an extension of a metre, a centimetre, or a millimetre, etc. Strictly speaking, all that is required is the presentation of something universal, without any individual determination. We have already seen that such a universal presentation is possible, when we saw that we do not appear to ourselves as individuated. We must add, however, that if a boundary forms part of a continuum – of which it constitutes the boundary – and is presented as such, then this continuum does not have to be presented *in modo recto* but only in *modo obliquo*.[84]

34 It has recently been denied that we inwardly perceive ourselves as being present, and even though this might seem rather strange to the layman, this denial is nothing but the necessary consequence of the attempt to classify temporal determination, like local ones, as differences in the objects rather than differences in the modes with which they are presented.[85] If 'present' denoted a special property as local determinations do, then we would have to say that the present almost certainly does not exist.[86] Only inner perception is evident, and thus it would be impossible for it to show us something as being present. All these difficulties are eliminated, however, when we recognize that temporal modes are not differences in the objects, but differences in the modes of presentation; and thus it cannot mislead us, but serves as an argument that our doctrine of the temporal modes is irrefutable.

35 But what about the mental as primary object? Does it appear

only in the *modus praesens* or does it also appear with other modes, perhaps even in a whole continuity of temporal modes? If I remember something, then I regard my own experience as a past one, I think of it as being at different distances – perhaps years away – from the present. And if I plan to do something in the future, then I have a presentation of something mental that belongs in the distant future. This might give rise to the belief that something mental is presented with a much larger continuous manifold[87] of temporal modes than if I see something at rest or in motion.

Yet if we look at this phenomenon more closely we will realize that we often have doubts concerning past experiences, i.e. we are often not sure which ones took place earlier and which ones later. Thus more recent experience does not appear to us in a different temporal mode from the one in which more distant experience appears to us, as should be the case if it corresponded to the course of history. We can, furthermore, see that a person who talks about an earlier experience 'relives it', so to speak, in the present. Thus we arrive at the knowledge that, in speaking of earlier experiences, no temporal modes are used other than those that we use when we intuit non-mental things. Thus one experience is associated in our minds with another, according to the temporal sequences of the experiences.[88] Insignificant events are passed over, and every new event seems to occur in the present mode. But then, as in other cases, the manifold of temporal modes seems to connect the event most recently spoken about with the one which was mentioned immediately prior to it in a kind of continual time sequence.

36   What we have considered so far belongs in the sensory realm; in addition to this realm we have distinguished an intelligible (intellective) one and here, too, we juxtaposed primary and secondary objects. Among the primary objects we listed, pre-eminently, the non-mental ones. Such an object is supposed to be given if we think of something white or red or something of a different colour, in abstraction from a specific place. Thanks to this abstraction the object is a universal one. The abstraction is supposed to go even further and enable us to think of something coloured in general apart from specific differences. The abstraction could also occur in another manner: it could pick out the local determination, either only *in specie* or only *in genere*, apart from all qualifications. And thus one can also think of certain species of extension and shape in an abstract manner. Here, too, it is commonly believed – when dealing with a specific local determination – that we are dealing with general objects, even though this is doubtful in those cases where

two things cannot interpenetrate locally.[89] It is also believed that one can abstract from quality and place and thus arrive at the concept of a thing in general.[90]

37   Yet there is no agreement on this point. Many philosophers deny altogether the possibility of such conceptual abstractions. Some have gone so far as to maintain that we cannot think of anything general, but only of particulars.[91] Our earlier discussions prove that this theory is incorrect. We have seen that not even in inner perception, i.e. not even in the sensory realm, do we comprehend ourselves according to our individual differences. Furthermore, the view that there exist only general terms but no general concepts is a contradiction in itself, since a term can only be called general, if there is a general concept that corresponds to it. If we deny this and say that a term is general if many individual presentations are associated with it, then we would misinterpret the difference between ambiguity and generality, and would fail to see that the statement that many individual presentations are associated with one and the same term, in itself expresses a general proposition concerning these individual presentations. Furthermore, it would require a whole multitude of proofs to prove the truth of a general proposition; each one of these proofs would correspond to an object falling under the general term. This would be utterly impossible. Thinking in general concepts, however, allows for a single proof.

38   Another question is whether without at the same time having a sensory intuition, we are able to think of the universals that we have acquired by means of abstraction, which is not only the source of these universals, but continues to bring them to our intuition. We might conclude that this is not necessary, because of the fact that we think of ourselves in general concepts, without having individually determined intuitions. Furthermore, experience shows that if we think of the concept of a triangle in general, it is by no means necessary to think of a specific individual triangle at the same time. On the contrary, it is just as impossible to intuit a straight line as it is to draw one, because there will always be certain irregularities. Thus it certainly is not true that a person who thinks the concept of a house in general has at the same time an intuitive presentation of a specific individual house or even of one side of it, or that he has a clearly determined presentation of the sizes of the individual parts of the house. Quite obviously just the opposite is true. The alleged experiences to the contrary can be explained by the fact that, when we think of a house or a triangle in general terms, we only do this by combining attributes, all of which originated in intuition.[92] In

addition, we usually think of the complicated concepts which are associated with the terms in a rather incomplete manner. It suffices that the elements that are not actually thought of come to mind, if, in the course of thinking about the matter, it becomes necessary to actually think of them. This will become clear immediately, if we raise the following question: when we speak of the state or the church, are we really conscious of the entire range of conceptual elements included in these concepts?[93] I mention this only in passing, since it would be more appropriate to carry out a more thorough investigation in a different context.[94] All that is important here is to establish the existence of so-called intelligible objects.[95]

39   We need no elaborate proof to show that − as in the case of sensory presentations of non-mental objects − here, too, in the realm of intelligible objects, there are additional presentations which take the intellective activities themselves as their objects. They are given as secondary, and sometimes[96] also as primary objects. There is a thoroughgoing analogy between the two areas.

40   If we now consider, however, that we also think of sensory and intelligible objects as combined, and if we ask which realm this act of combining falls under, then we are slightly at a loss: sensory and intellective activities seem to be united here. The sensory activities constitute a prerequisite for the intellective ones, while the latter are not a prerequisite for the former; thus it is clear that such cases do not generally fall into the sensory realm.

41   The objects which we acquire through abstraction are, to a greater or lesser extent, general. The question is whether we arrive at the most general concepts, i.e. whether one particular concept will turn out to be the most general one, or whether we arrive at many general concepts that differ from each other, but which do not allow for further generalization.[97]

II

A MORE DETAILED DISCUSSION OF THE PROCESS OF ABSTRACTION AND THE UNIVERSAL NATURE OF PERCEPTION AND SENSATION[1]

1   There is no agreement as to whether or not we think general ideas, i.e. universals and if so how we do it – whether we do it independently or in relation to individual things, i.e. particulars, the intuition of which includes the thinking of general ideas. Nor is there agreement as to whether the general ideas, which we think, correspond to existing things. Nor do those who answer affirmatively all agree among themselves; some maintain that only individuals correspond to the general, while others maintain that in addition to individuals there is also something which has no individual determination.

2   Each of the conflicting opinions mentioned above has its adherents even today. That does not mean, however, that some have not already been definitively refuted. Aristotle pointed out that only individuals exist and that there is nothing indeterminate and general that exists independently of and in addition to them. The beliefs that we cannot think of universals,[2] and that so-called general terms are only associated with a multitude of individual presentations, have also been refuted. This would make them equivocal terms and a single proof for a truth expressed in general terms would be impossible. Any mathematical theorem will serve to refute this. Berkeley, who called himself a nominalist, was not a nominalist in the strict sense of the word, for he did not deny outright that we have general ideas; all he denied is that we think them in a different way than we think something individual. This, however, is exactly what a number of realists of the Middle Ages taught, and they believed themselves to be in agreement with Aristotle. What Aristotle actually means is that when we think a concept which is an

abstraction from an intuition, we must always present an intuition which is included in the concept, in order to be able to understand the concept in connection with the intuition. This was a generalization of one of Plato's doctrines, which states that we can comprehend and calculate geometric figures in general only with reference to the individual instances which we present.

3 Aristotle, however, believed that the accidents are individualized by means of the substance whose accidents they are, i.e. they are individualized by means of the individual determination of the substance. The inevitable consequence is that a person who does not have a presentation of the individual determination of the substance cannot think of either the substance or the accident in terms other than universal ones. Because Aristotle believed further that we cannot comprehend a substance in any other than its most general concept, it follows, according to him, that all our presentations, including sensory intuitions, are actually presentations of something universal.[3]

4 If we leave the teachings of this great philosopher aside, one thing still seems certain, namely, that no one is able to indicate what it is that individuates him as a thinking being. What he sees, hears, tastes, believes, denies, wishes, wants, enjoys, feels sad about, etc., could very well, with no contradiction whatsoever, be the objects of any number of other people. Thus nothing can be regarded as more certain than the fact that in no case is self-knowledge completely determined knowledge which includes the individuating determination. We are, thus, dealing here with a general presentation which is given without reference to individual intuitions.[4]

5 Let us investigate other cases. Is it true, as Aristotle believed, that in sensory intuition we intuit only something general as primary object? If it is certain that more than one body cannot be in the same place at the same time, then one might conclude that whatever appears localized in sensory intuition thus appears to be individualized. Yet if we concentrate on the 'at the same time' we could often argue in the opposite way: several things can appear, one after the other, in one and the same place. And are we not forced to say that temporal determinations themselves are real differences? If this is the case, it would seem that the statement that we intuit something individual would be applicable only in those instances where what is intuited appears with a temporal determination. This, however, is not the case. The differences between present, past and more distant past indicate nothing that would be applicable to every time element at one point or another and we do not know the special

characteristic of the very time element that is present at this particular moment, nor that it belongs to a certain extent to the past or the future. A certain degree of indeterminacy of the phenomenon thus cannot be denied in this case, either, and this gives us a certain justification for speaking of universality.[5]

6   A close investigation thus reveals that only what is general can be the object of our thought and this is quite contrary to the doctrine of the nominalists. There are, however, degrees of generality, and, as concerns external sensory perception, which lacks [only][6] temporal determination, we certainly approach complete individuation.[7] Our thinking is much further removed from complete individuation when we think of a triangle, a circle, a two-dimensional figure, a planimetric figure, a figure, an area, a body, a line, a point, a boundary, something red, something coloured, something with sensible qualities, etc. We have already pointed out that this is the case, yet also said the question how we think these things warrants further investigation. Some philosophers have maintained that such thinking presupposes sensory intuition. It was maintained that general ideas are abstracted from sensory intuitions. But what is this process of abstraction? The linguistic expression seems to indicate that that which is abstracted is contained in that which is sensorily intuited – that we intuit it implicitly at the same time. Yet it is certain that we cannot differentiate, in a sensory manner, between points straight lines, circles and lines in general or between boundaries in general. So people then said it is not sense but reason which abstracts. This, however, hardly tells us anything positive. If we examine the following case more closely it also seems to be false to say that the geometer has a general idea of a triangle when looking at an individual triangle that is drawn in the sand, because the so-called triangle that is drawn in the sand is not actually a triangle. Not a single one of its sides is a genuinely straight line; not a single one of its so-called angles has a genuine apex, an indispensable characteristic of an angle. In the same way, a so-called circle drawn in the sand is not actually a circle. There is no doubt that drawing such a geometric figure in the sand is an important aid to the geometer,[8] otherwise he would not use it; yet this figure, being something individuated or at least approaching individuation, cannot serve as an example for concepts with a higher degree of generality. It is quite natural to conceive the function of this geometric figure as one of *serving as a guideline for the association of thought-determinations*[9] which are included in the general thought if this thought were actually thought in complete manner, which, however, is

not always the case. Then the function would appear to be similar to that of a name. If we say the name of God, we think of something with which a variety of attributes is associated, these attributes do not always actually come to mind, yet the habitual use of the name makes their appearance more likely. If something is said that constitutes a contradiction to one of the attributes of God, then the attribute concerned will immediately enter into our actual act of thinking, causing us to reject the contradictory thought. Yet it would be absurd to maintain that the attributes of God are implicitly contained in the name itself.

It is also interesting to note that geometers have recently been concerned with proofs of theorems that deal not just with bodies or the boundaries of such bodies, but with four-dimensional topoids, of which we have and can have no sensory intuitions, even though some people have believed that they do. Therefore, they have thought the concept of a four-dimensional topoid without having any intuition of it; this allows us to conclude with certainty that concepts of a three-dimensional body,[10] or a sphere, a cube, a circle, etc. can also be thought in general without being comprehended in a sensory intuition. Nevertheless, certain abstractions from sensory intuitions seem to be an indispensable prerequisite, although in an utterly different way.[11]

7   Let us now devote some time to another class of general concepts. I mean sensory, qualitative concepts such as the concept of something blue, red, black, white, something coloured in general, sounds, and sounds of a particular pitch and tone colour, etc., etc. The concept of something red is more general than the intuition of a red patch[12] which I see somewhere in my field of vision, and the concept seems abstract in respect to it. But how does this happen? Is a completely red spot clearly differentiated in our intuition? Or is it that which we differentiate and clearly notice at one time white, at another time black or grey or yellow or blue or something else? We call something black and then find that it is not black to the same extent as something else which is even blacker. If, on the basis of such experiences someone begins to doubt whether he has ever intuitively distinguished a perfect black, we must ask how he arrived at his standard and how he formed this concept of pure black. If someone shows us something violet, we say that it is bluish and reddish; psychology ventures even further and maintains[13] that we must have infinitesimally small spots of pure red and pure blue in our intuition in order to be able to see something violet. But nobody can say of a specific spot that it is at that very moment pure red or pure blue. If nothing pure

red can be apprehended in the intuition, it seems paradoxical to believe that we can abstract the concept of pure red from it. On the basis of what we have said so far, this same paradox arises with regard to all colour intuitions. We can say something analogous with regards to sounds. Despite that, however, these paradoxes do not give rise to any doubt concerning the fact that our general qualitative concepts have their origin in the realm of sensorily qualified intuitions.

It is certain that we do not notice everything which is presented in an intuition, and we do not differentiate and characterize with complete precision those aspects which we do notice. Yet this incompleteness does not prevent us from making some distinctions and comparisons in which one thing in relation to another is recognized as being the same or similar, or more or less similar than some third thing. And this brings us to the idea of something in which they participate equally or to a greater or lesser degree, and, further, to the idea of an even greater approximation to the highest possible degree of possession of this property. In this manner we can explain quite well how we arrive at the concept of pure red, even though all the red things that we can see include small particles of blue or yellow or black or white or a mixture of some of these colours, so that we cannot differentiate a pure red particle as such. It also explains how we can form the concept of something coloured in general from having recognized the differences between coloured objects, although always in a confused way. Something similar happens when, having observed physical continua, one coloured, the other qualified by some warm or cold temperature or other, we thereby arrive at the concept of a physical continuum which is an abstraction from colour as well as temperature. And even though we are not able to distinguish every individual little particle in an intuitive continuum – we are not even sure that this continuum does not contain small gaps at various places – we will still be able to differentiate in a rough way the parts of this continuum and thus recognize the existence of the general character of a physical continuum. We are even less able to distinguish a precise individual boundary line or an exact point and see them as parts of infinitesimally small size in any dimension. Yet we do sufficiently recognize that that which we see has an extension. And by differentiating larger and smaller parts of this extension we arrive at the concept of diminishing size, i.e., the extension is divided in half, and each half is again divided in half, and so forth. Thus we can make the final boundary area of the physical continuum as small as we like, while the body itself appears unchanged with regard to the end of the continuum.

Thus we arrive at the concept of a surface, as well as the concept of areas that form the inner boundaries between parts which form boundaries on both sides, and consequently we arrive at the concepts of lines as the outer or inner boundaries of an area, and at the concept of points as boundaries of a line, an area, and a body. As concerns the point, the thought of a diminuation into infinity with respect to every dimension occurs, and we see that even if we think of the point as being located in one and the same place, it still has a certain universality in so far as we think of it as the boundary of a continuum with a certain, but not specified, extension.[14] The point retains this kind of universality even when it is indicated whether or not the point is a boundary on all sides, or if it is an external boundary point which forms a boundary only on certain sides. For in any case we can think of the extension of that which is bounded as being as small as we like. All that is said is that it also has a certain extension in the third dimension. If we are dealing with a concept such as that of a straight line, then we will easily see from what has been said that the process of formation is a complicated one. We do not simply comprehend the general concept of a straight line by means of a comparison between several individual straight lines which we have distinguished in the continuum; rather, only after we have arrived at the concept of the line and at the concept of a more or less irregular course of lines, will we reach the extreme, i.e., lines with a regular course, a course which is changed neither suddenly nor gradually, neither to a greater nor to a lesser degree, lines whose direction in fact never changes, so that every intermediate point on the line lies precisely between the two terminal points.

This, then, is the procedure and those who called it abstraction, really had no sufficiently clear idea of it. In addition to distinguishing and comparing, other processes also came into play such as the continual approximating of an extreme and a multiple inference process.[15] The result is not a concept of intuitive unity, but a complicated thought which relates many things that are thought of *in modo recto* and *in modo obliquo* to one another.[16]

8   The above comments on the processes which lead to the thinking of universals show that we can never reach them without thinking of something relative. Even the very simplest cases require drawing comparisons. We thereby recognize agreement and difference. And, of course, an act of thinking is impossible without a relation to that which we think. If we think that something is in conformity with something else, then we think one thing *in recto* and the other thing *in obliquo*.

Some philosophers, however, have wanted to go so far as to classify all universals themselves as relative. They said red means being specifically equal in redness to something else, coloured means being generically equal in colour to something else. This belief, however, is utterly wrong. For a thing to be red it is not necessary that something else must be red, too. If something else is red and ceases to be red then this does not mean that the first thing ceases to be red, too, because the relation of agreement is no longer present. If red were a relation, then one and the same thing would have the property of redness as many times as there were things that agreed with it in redness. Thus it is very important to differentiate between the statement that an agreement in redness or a similarity due to mutual approximation to pure red is recognized in the process of abstraction, and the statement that the thought of red itself is the thought of something which is equal in redness to something else.

9   On the basis of our observations we will have to reject as unfounded and erroneous the claim that the comparison which is necessary between a number of red things on the occasion of the first formation of the thought of red must be repeated every time we subsequently think of red. What actually happens is that a certain disposition remains which makes it possible for us to recognize the red in everything red or reddish that we encounter. Also the other processes which occur in connection with more complicated cases appear to be shortened and simplified once the complicated concept has been formed, so that this concept is associated with the general names even though not always with all their characteristics; it is immediately available for use in the manner described above.[17]

10   The question arises whether, when we can repeat the act of thinking of a universal at which we arrived by way of abstraction it is necessary to have an intuition similar to the one from which the universal stemmed.[18]

11   Another difficulty must be dealt with. We said that, if we examine them closely, all our presentations are characterized by a degree of indeterminateness which in turn endows them with a certain character of universality. How is it possible, then, that we are nevertheless convinced that we are always dealing with individuals and not with something general that stands by itself, nor even with a multitude of individual things falling under the same concept. This question arises in connection with self-knowledge. We proved that that which distinguishes our individuality from that of any other human being does not appear to us. How do we know that it is a single mind

and not many individual ones which we comprehend in inner perception? The answer is that nothing can be perceived with direct evidence as being purely factual unless it is identical with the perceiving being. For only such an identity could lead to contradiction if that which is affirmed by the affirming being did not exist.[19] Yet no individual can be identical with more than one individual, and thus an individual cannot perceive with direct evidence more than one individual, namely himself. As I pointed out before, it is not impossible that there are still any number of individual things which, regardless of the differences due to individualizing determinations, are like this individual being in that they perceive themselves, in that they do this with the same degree of uncertainty and in that they comprehend themselves in exactly the same manner as I do. Every one of them comprehends a single other individual thing which falls under the same universal determinations according to which I comprehend myself.[20]

We encounter an essentially similar situation with the sensory intuition of external objects. We said that something is missing which keeps them from being fully individually determined, namely the characteristic of specific temporal determination[21] which is different for every event that occurs at an earlier or later point in the course of things; and this specificity does not appear with regard to things which we intuit as being present or past. Everything present appears absolutely the same if it appears as being present. This is very true, but it is also true that two events that are separated by a temporal distance cannot both exist. If in the course of time one event were to occur several times in exactly the same manner except for the temporal determination, it would be impossible for more than one to exist. Thus no more than one (thing) could exist which corresponds to our intuition.[22]

12   This leads to another important question, a question which must be regarded as particularly difficult, for philosophers have tried to solve it for thousands of years, and have never managed to come to any agreement. St. Augustine dealt with it in his *Confessions*. 'What then is time?' He says, 'I know well enough what it is provided that nobody asks me; but if I am asked what it is ... I am baffled.'[23] One thing is certain, just as in the case of space, we are dealing with a continuum of things next to each other, analogously in the case of time, we have a continuum of things following one after the other. In connection with space, things which are next to each other both exist, but in the case of time we must say that if the earlier exists, the later does not, and if the later exists the earlier does not. The continual temporal process exists

only in connection with a boundary. Another point causes difficulties. If we ask how we arrive at the idea of something that has spatial extension, we must answer that everything which we see or externally perceive with some other sense appears not only as sensorily qualified, but also as spatially extended. This leads to an abstraction of the spatially specifically determined[24] from the sensory qualification and to an abstraction of the general concept of the spatial in that which is located next to something else and that which is separated from something else.

What about the temporal realm? The immediate conclusion would be that here we have an analogous situation, i.e. that external and inner perception (or one of the two) shows us temporal continua in specific temporal determination together with some other determinations; that we abstract, by means of comparison, first that which is temporally specifically determined from all heterogenous determinations, and then arrive at the general concept of the temporal continuum, i.e. the contiguity and distance between that which is earlier or later. Yet a closer examination reveals that this assumption is incompatible with the facts. If a particular temporal span were to appear in its peculiar specific determinations, then only one of these determinations could exist; all others, however, would either be non-existent or impossible. Therefore, it is hard to believe that this impossibility would not become obvious[25] if we really had a presentation of these determinations. Furthermore, by analogy with the spatial visual field, we would have to assume that the specific temporal determinations which appear would always appear in the same manner. This shows the correctness of the statement that the moment which appears to us as present and in whose existence we believe, seems to be modified by other determinations such as the peculiarities of instantaneous thinking, feeling, etc., but not, however, modified in a temporal sense. Every present, as such, appears to be the same. The real temporal determinations, however, must constantly change; and thus the contrast between appearance and reality is undeniable in this case. Yet in contrast to spatial determinations, which can be attributed only to bodies, temporal determinations are attributable to all things, material or immaterial. Thus it must be obvious that if a specific temporal determination appears in external intuition, it must also appear in inner perception. Inner perception, however, is infallible; for this reason the temporal determination would always have to appear in a different manner in inner perception just as surely as it does in reality. Yet this is not the case, thus we clearly realize that a specific temporal determination is not given in inner appearance.[26]

In opposition to this it has been suggested that it is not as inconvenient as it appears that only the phenomena of external perception exhibit temporal determinations. After all, it is only here that we encounter a continual series which extends from something present to something past. When we hear a word, for example, the component sounds appear as past at the end of the word, while we ourselves think of one sound as belonging to the more distant past, and another as belonging to the more recent past. Well-known philosophers have regarded the phenomenon of time as a special characteristic of inner sense, and if it is true that pain and pleasure belong to the realm of inner sense, then it seems to be rather obvious that mental things, too, appear continually, alternatingly, and as prior or subsequent to each other. If we comprehend prior and subsequent only on the basis of the intuition of different special temporal determinations, then the realm of inner sense will also contain phenomena of such temporal determinations and this will also apply, in particular, to the moment which exists and which is comprehended with the evidence of inner experience.[27]

As mentioned above, we saw, and the result of our discussion justifies, that our inner as well as our external intuitions are characterized by a certain degree of indeterminacy and generality in so far as they lack any special temporal determination.

13   How, then, was it possible for us to acquire the concepts which have to do with the temporal?

There are philosophers who teach that we are wholly restricted to the relative, with regard both to knowledge and even to presentation. According to them we sense a colour only in relation to other colours, a sound only in relation to other sounds, we think of a length only in relation to other lengths, etc. From the point of view of these philosophers we would have to say that we comprehend something temporal only in relation to other temporal things, that we never have an absolute presentation of any of these; consequently we would have a presentation of a before and an after, but not of any absolute temporal difference. Accordingly we would call something past or future only in relation to something present. The same applies to something belonging to the more distant or more recent past, or to the more immediate or remote future. We would undoubtedly find abundant examples of these relative aspects in our intuitions of changes of location or the succession of notes in a melody. Whoever demands more in connection with time, e.g., whoever wants proof of absolute time differences that would be attributed to the present moment or to yesterday, demands something that is utterly impossible, something which, in an analogous manner, is utterly impossible with regard to space, colour and sound – in other words with regard to everything which we have presentations of or know. All that is required here is the knowledge that there are certain limits to our presentation, in order to counteract the opinion that something special is missing here which necessitates further research. Here, as in other cases, we have only relative determinations, and for these intuitions from which they are abstracted are clear and distinct.

14   No matter how popular the above-mentioned relativity theory is, it is simply not true. We have pointed out above that we cannot acquire the general concepts of red and of colour without comparisons and the activity of making them, but once we have acquired them we can actually think them again and again without making comparisons – a statement which would be incompatible with the belief that they are merely relations.[28] Quite in contrast to what has been maintained above with such great conviction, a better psychology would make us realize that if we did not have absolute presentations, we could never arrive at a presentation of something relative that would determine one in comparison with another. A confusion of two completely different questions has led to the false doctrine discussed above. It is quite a different matter to ask whether we always need to know absolute number and lengths in order to establish relations of numbers and of lengths, and to ask whether, having no absolute concepts of number and lengths but acquiring them from intuition, we are able to think those relative concepts at all. If someone maintains that we only need the concepts of double and half, but not those of one and two in order to recognize that one amount is twice as large as another – because that does not mean that we have 1 on the one side and 2 on the other – then we would immediately reject this statement as silly. And if the proponents of the doctrine say that we cannot be conscious of a sound without a multitude of sound presentations, then this completely wrong proposition could even be called absurd if we did not understand by this multitude of sounds a multitude of absolute sounds.[29] It is never possible to have a presentation of comparative relation *in specie* without having a presentation *in specie* of the absolute determinations, the comparative relation of which is important here. Furthermore, it is impossible to have a presentation of a comparative relation *in genere* without having a presentation *in genere* of that between which it is to be found.[30]

Aristotle's judgment is much more correct than those of some modern philosophers. He did not say that in those cases where we see nothing but white no colours appear at all; he said only that we cannot move from the concept of white to the general concept of something coloured, so that for us white and coloured would simply coincide. Furthermore, we would have no ideas of intervals between colours, as between black and white, red and blue. Yet we do talk of temporal intervals; thus it seems undeniable that we have a presentation of different temporal species analogous to the different colour species, and we are justified in asking where we get them.[31]

15   In order to answer this question, it will be necessary to point out the important difference which appears in comparing things that are temporally sequential. If we compare things that are spatially separate, then the fundament and the terminus both exist in the same way. If we compare, however, things that are separated by a temporal interval, when the fundament exists the terminus does not.[32] Yet this case is not similar to that of a thought's relation to its object, where very often the object of the thought has no actuality.[33] If something truly is earlier or later than something else, then it is not earlier or later than this other thing is, but, rather, earlier or later than this other thing was or will be. The more thorough the investigation, the clearer it will become that, while it is true that we recognize the fundament and the terminus by means of same mode of affirmation with regard to things next to each other, we must point out, in connection with sequences, that the modes of affirmation are different for each thing in the sequence. These modes, however, are not like the assertoric and apodictic modes, where the latter include the former.[34] A closer examination reveals that these modes are already there in cases of mere presentations, for example, of movements, states of rest or a succession of tones.[35] Both with regard to time and space we have, regardless of the differences as to the object, another kind of difference which belongs to the content of the presentation of the temporal;[36] and it is this difference and not the former which differentiates the present from the past and the future, or from a more or less distant past, etc. If it is true, as pointed out above, that there is difference with respect to the object in the case of sequences, as is the case with positions next to each other in the spatial realm, it is not impossible that we fail to find this difference included in the presentations. This would mean that the temporal differentiation of presentations would, in our case, be limited to the difference between the temporal modes.[37] If this is the actual case – and I have no doubt that it is and have already said so – and if it leads to that kind of universality which we have discussed before, then we no longer need to explain the

origin of that which does not exist at all.[38] It suffices to clarify how, by observing our modes of presentation, we arrive at the concepts of something to be presented as belonging to the present, the past, the more immediate and the more distant past, the future, of something earlier and something later. This should suffice for the conclusion of our discussion of universals. We discussed the theory of the temporal modes in more detail elsewhere and there we showed in what the transcendent temporal object-differences must consist.[39]

III

THE KNOWLEDGE OF THE TEMPORAL ABSOLUTE AND ITS SPECIES[1]

1   If inner perception is evident, then we have a basis for deciding the question of its extent.[2]

2   Thus we can prove, for example, that it does not give us any clue as to whether or not our thoughts are changing within us.

3   Naturally, this is compatible with the fact that it says that *we believe* that such a change takes place. This belief will not then itself be the evidence of inner perception.

4   Let us assume that God puts us in a state of suspended animation for an hour (which he undoubtedly can do), at a moment in which we are listening to a melody or speech and at which we have very vivid visual impressions of dance movements. All of these as well as all other intentional relations would remain unchanged for a whole hour; we would be in complete teleiosis[3] as concerns our thinking throughout this hour. The impression of a vivid mental change which we have at the first moment of such a state of rest would continue unchanged during that whole hour. No psychologist would deny this.*

---

*The Psychological Realists believe in the truth of external perception. Yet if we perceive a succession of sounds, one sound appears as past while another one seems to be present, and it is impossible that this appearance always be true, if that which appears as past appears at a certain temporal distance from the present. All that could happen would be that the sound which appears as past alternatingly recurs as present and then returns again to the old distance from the sound which appears as present for the second time. On the other hand it would be quite feasible, without giving rise to any contradiction, that the mental state would persist, in which case the sound which appears to me as past would appear permanently at the same distance from the present, without my being conscious of it.

This would be a new and rather impressive argument against psychological realism.[4]

5   Since inner perception would thus show us as we actually are, it seems that it would have to show us in our present state as belonging to a temporal continuum. Even in a state of complete rest, our existence is a coming into being and passing away in the sense that that which passes away, leaving aside the differentiation which forms an integral part of the flow of time, merely regenerates itself regularly. The specific difference of times that follow one after the other remains completely hidden due to the generality with which we comprehend our substance, which is first concerned with it. All we can conclude is that there must be a specific difference, in the same way as we infer the necessity of specific substantial differences in us without perceiving a single one. What we do perceive is the difference between something appearing to us as present, and something else as somehow past or future. Consequently, we perceive that a thing (which not only hears, but also believes that it heard, which not only sees but also believes that it saw) appears in a state of transition from a past state to a present one and its present state forms the boundary of the past. This is due to the fact that the difference between the present state and the state just gone by can, in every respect, only be an infinitesimal one. Yet inner perception cannot tell us whether such an infinitesimal difference is given at all in any relation other than the intuition of time. If we also generally believe in it, as in the above case, then this belief is a blind one, as are memory beliefs in general.[5]

6   We can now ask whether, as a consequence of the generality with which we inwardly comprehend ourselves, we are at all conscious in inner perception of the fact that our existence is a continuum and, as a boundary of such, exists in reality? And if we could conceive of things that did not exist in time, then we would have to accept this[6] as being correct, because of the extreme generality with which we appear to ourselves. Yet this is not the case; on the contrary, temporality is a general characteristic of all things, just as spatiality is a general characteristic of all bodies. Thus we must also comprehend ourselves in inner perception as a boundary of a temporal continuum, but without knowing any more about this continuum than is generally attributed to a continuum; so that with the activities through which we perceive ourselves in ourselves, we are able to form a boundary for that which, as pointed out above, is possible in such a varied manner and in complete as well as incomplete teleiosis.[7]

7   The only indication that inner perception seems to give us concerning the length of the past is that it must have had some length.

8   How can we understand this far-reaching indeterminacy?

Perhaps we will arrive at an explanation if we consider that nothing can be thought of as past if we do not simultaneously think of something as present. If we think this present as being though *in modo recto* and the past *in modo obliquo* in other relations, but also with regard to the distance from the present and with regard to its temporal extension. In general, we could ask if we should not attribute all temporal modes of the past and the future to the *modis obliquis* of presenting; in which case, the temporal mode of the present would simply be identified[8] with the *modus rectus* of presenting.

9   Special attention should be devoted to the question of the case where I speak of something existing at sometime or other, where this sometime or other includes not only the past and the future, but also the present. It seems, however, that simultaneity is a temporal relation just as earlier and later are. And the concept of temporal relation to something present can be expressed in such general terms that it also includes simultaneity. Something existing sometime or other would then be that to which the present has some kind of temporal relation, and thus it would appear as being thought *in modus obliquus*.

IV

FURTHER INVESTIGATION OF THE UNIVERSALITY OF ALL INTUITIONS – IN PARTICULAR SPATIAL AND TEMPORAL INTUITIONS AND THE TEMPORAL ABSOLUTE UNIVERSALS[1]

1   If we ask whether our thinking is ever directed[2] towards universal objects,[2] we must answer yes.

2   We think of universals not because there exists something in reality which lacks individual determination, but because we think something that is individually determined in such a general way that several individually determined things do or can correspond to our thought.[3] This is precisely the reason we say that the objects of thought are universal.

3   The Ultra-Realists violate the above-mentioned principles. Some, such as Plato, believe in independently existing universals, while others, such as William of Champeaux, maintain that the universal does not exist independently but in the individual things: logical parts, the same in all individuals that fall under the same general concept. Thus we could not speak of a multiplication of them in relation to the number of the individuals. One individual thing would suffice for their coming into being, and thus they would appear to be independent as regards every other individual. It is not difficult to see that this theory contains a number of contradictions.[4]

4   Yet the so-called Nominalists violate the former stipulation by denying that we have general thoughts at all. It is said that we only use general names, i.e. names with which we associate a number of meanings. The only difference between them and accidentally ambiguous names would be the fact that the various things that are associated with the name are similar to each other.

Yet this view, too, is easily refutable. According to this theory there would be no universal concepts, no universal judgments and no universal syllogistic conclusions.

We could never have a proof that would be applicable to all triangles; it would require an infinite induction, the result of which would still not render a single universal law, but only an infinite multitude of different cognitions.

5   Yet it is a different matter if we ask whether or not we can arrive at universal concepts independently of individual presentation.

Indeed, we arrive at the concept of something coloured usually only by means of abstraction from white, red, blue or other specifically coloured things, and Aristotle maintains that we never think of something coloured in general without at the same time having a presentation of a certain coloured thing, even though the concept acquired earlier by means of abstraction is repeated. Some thinkers even maintain that in every instance – at the time of the first acquisition as well as at the time of the repetition – several coloured things must be presented and compared.

Without going into the question of whether this is proved or not, it would not appear to be absurd for it to be otherwise.[5]

The act of thinking that relates to something coloured in general is different from the act of thinking, whose object is something of a specific colour, and the latter is not included in the former.

This becomes even clearer in cases where we think of something universal which we did not acquire by means of abstraction from something less general (or something individual).[6] Inner perception is such a case. If I perceive myself inwardly, I do not perceive anything which could not also be characteristic of many other thinking beings. Everything that I perceive here could also be perceived by another being. That which individuates me does not appear in my inner perception. As far as substance is concerned, I recognize myself only as a thing. If this were different, then there would be no dispute between materialists and idealists at all.[7]

6   Since it is no doubt true that nothing which we perceive in inner perception is individually determined, and what we perceive is perceived without having a corresponding individual presentation at the same time, we must ask if this could not be applied to any universal concept without giving rise to contradictions. Why should it be possible with regard to substance and not possible with regard to accidental determinations? After all, the hearing being appears to be specified as

hearing being, but not individualized. (Even if I hear one certain sound, I do not appear individualized. All accidents lack individuation.)[8]

Wouldn't it also be possible to have universal relative concepts without having a presentation of specifically determined relative concepts and their specifically determined fundaments and termini? We can think that something is larger than something else without thinking of the specific sizes of either. We can hardly deny *a priori* the possibility of such independent, relative, universal concepts.

7   This calls for an investigation of the question of whether or not we actually have experience of some such cases. Indeed, it seems that – in connection with spatial determination – nothing that is specifically and logically differentiated can be thought, while we can very well have presentations of spatial distances and connections in the realm of the three-dimensional. This is how Leibniz arrived at his doctrine that space consists of nothing but relations, and location is attributed to a body or part of a body only on the basis of its spatial distances from other bodies – it being closer or farther away. He said that, therefore, one could neither speak of a difference between the location of the world as a whole and the location of other possible worlds nor of God preferring one above the other.

This would hardly be understandable if Leibniz had found the presentation of absolute spatial differences in intuition and experience. What is more, Newton, who held a different opinion in this respect, arrived at it only gradually. There were special reasons which led him to assume that there are absolute spatial determinations. (We know that reflections on certain consequences of the rotation of a sphere around its axis caused Newton to assume the existence of an absolute space. He asked himself, what is the cause of the protuberance at the equator due to the rotation of the earth.) Yet Newton's doubt could hardly be understood if he had found absolute local differences in intuition.

Modern physicists in general have returned to the Leibnizian view. They deny all absolute local determinations or at least they consider them unproved, they only speak of relative location and relative states of rest and motion.

8   If, then, all these considerations are correct, what about our external perception?

Empiricists attempt to deny altogether that local determinations have been connected from the outset with qualities. Rather we associate them only on the basis of experience. The nativists oppose this. They maintain that – as specific energies – absolute local determinations are usually connected with the qualities. This forced them to claim that not all absolute local determinations which are revealed to us by the senses correspond to those of the things in the external world which cause our sensations. The former appear the same wherever we are in the world, and if they exist in reality there might be a distance of millions and trillions of miles between them and us. We employ them only with regard to the local relations which they show and which make it possible to form concepts of arbitrarily larger and smaller distances.

If the assumption is possible that a presentation contains only relative and not final[9] absolute determinations, wouldn't it be more convenient to assume that this was actually the case with regard to our sensory intuition? Then this strange constant pretence of certain infinitely distant places would become superfluous.[10] We would intuit only universals[11] but it was the same with inner perception so there is no reason for us to feel uncomfortable about this.

9   In addition, we gain a tremendously significant advantage. The question which we have raised in connection with space, i.e. whether we present only relative or also absolute determinations, recurs in connection with time. There, too, Leibniz believed that we are only dealing with relations. And thus, just as, if there is a spatially bounded world, God would not have to choose between positions at different places in space. He would not have to choose between different positions in time either if the whole course of the world had a beginning and an end, or at least a beginning. The development of such an opinion would be unthinkable if not only relative but also absolute temporal differences appeared in intuitions of successions, or states of motion and rest, or sequences of sounds. Here, too, every present seems to be exactly the same. Yet if it were to include an absolute specific temporal determination, it would have to change constantly, otherwise it would be a delusion – it would give us a false impression of something that existed perhaps millions of years ago or will exist in the future. All temporal determinations such as yesterday, a year ago, etc., clearly relate to the present. If our choice in connection with time is limited to the assumption that we have only presentations of relative temporal determinations, and the assumption that we have only wrong temporal determinations and, in particular, a wrong temporal determination of the present, then it is clear that we must tend towards the first assumption, because inner perception, too, shows something as being present, and inner perception is completely true and certain. Thus it is impossible that something false be contained in our temporal

determination of the present. The above statements provide a solution to a problem which otherwise would have been impossible to solve.

10   We have seen so far how our assumption that our inner and external intuitions contain only relative and not absolute local and temporal determinations is the only one that makes the theory of the mere relativity of space and time understandable – a theory which is adhered to by Leibniz and many other modern physicists. Even Newton and his followers do give it some consideration. This becomes even more important when we consider that those who do not believe in absolute places and times do not usually object when someone maintains that there would be no intervals between colours or sounds if there were no absolute colours and sounds. People usually maintain that colours and sounds can exist by themselves. This difference in judgment in the two cases is simply the consequence of the fact that intuition presents us with absolute colours and sounds, but not with absolute local and temporal differences. Even if it did show absolute specific local and temporal determinations, the fact that not truth *per se* but only so-called phenomenal truth can be attributed to them, would not suffice as explanation, since it is only phenomenal truth which is attributable to absolute colour and sound determinations as well. We have also pointed out that certain things that Aristotle says are connected with this. He uses only relative determinations to illustrate the categories of place and time: in the Lyceum, in the market, yesterday, a year ago. Another aspect of his theory becomes understandable in light of the above statements; at the point where he lists the common sensibles he does not speak of place and time, but of extension and shape, states of rest and motion, which can be the same regardless of place and time, as long as the local and temporal circumstances are the same. His view, therefore, goes hand in hand with the assumption that sensory intuition does not show absolute local and temporal differences, but only local and temporal relations.

11   Even though it seems to be more and more attractive to assume that our sensory intuition as well as our inner perception shows no absolute, but only relative, spatial and temporal determinations, we should not be tempted to follow Leibniz and many other modern thinkers who believe in nothing but the existence of relative local and temporal differences in reality. Here as in other cases of universal presentations of comparative relations, a thorough analysis will reveal that *absolute determinations are included in the general determinations*: ('something local, spatial', 'something temporal' is absolute, 'distance' is

relative), e.g., the presentation of something lighter or better includes the determination of lightness and goodness in general. Likewise, the presentation of something that has a spatial or temporal distance in a certain direction or to a certain extent includes the determination of space and time in general. Thus, just as the general concept of substance is contained in that which is inwardly perceived, the general concept of something temporal and of something spatial seems to be included in our inner and external[12] intuition respectively, if temporal or spatial relations are included therein. In opposition to the Ultra-Realists, however, we established that a universal reality cannot actually exist. Consequently, we do not actually encounter just spatial and temporal relations, but also absolute spatial and temporal differences which are specifically and individually determined.

12 If we ask, however, for the general concept of something spatial and something temporal we will have to note the following: the concept of something temporal coincides with the concept of the thing in so far as it is substantially determined, i.e. in so far as it includes a substance. What we are dealing with is the fact that every substance exists as boundary of a one-dimensional primary continuum, which does not exist according to any other of its boundaries and yet truly belongs to this very continuum[13] and is distant from any other of its boundaries in the sense of being earlier or later. This is a part of the concept of substance and thus also of the concept of everything, in so far as the accidents, too, include the general concept of substance. If we had absolute specific temporal determinations, they would constitute substantial specific differences in one of the series in which the universal species of substance is specifically differentiated.[14]

The universal species of something spatial has a small scope, and is attributed at first to the substantial things and through the substantial subject to their accidents as well. The spatial differences appear as specific differences of a certain category of substances which belong to a different series of the essential differentiation of substance in general – that to which the temporal differences belong. The substances which participate in it appear to belong thereby to a three-dimensional primary continuum, the *species specialissima* of which individualize the substance concerned. This continuum cannot only exist with respect to one, but with respect to innumerable of its boundaries. (Yet it is not impossible to conceive that it exists only with respect to one of its boundaries, if this boundary were only temporally connected with other boundaries and parts of a spatial continuum which is called its fourth dimension; with respect to which it would appear not only as primary but also as secondary continuum with time being the basis of the primary continuum. If we take a cone and, starting from its base, gradually destroy it, the cone would eventually only exist as a point. On the other hand, if the process of destruction began at the apex the cone would eventually exist only as the boundary of a plane figure.)

13   According to the empiricists, only relative determinations would be associated with external intuition. According to Guyot, who developed a temporal empiricism analogous to spatial empiricism the same would have to hold true of the temporal.

14   According to what has been said above, therefore, it is inherent in the concept of a thing to be connected with something real as something later and earlier, or at least as one of these, to belong to this real thing while the continuing real thing to which it belongs is not an earlier or later boundary. No definite extension, no event – no matter how small – is inherent in the general concept of a thing. For this reason, it is an inherent characteristic of this concept that it can be distinguished from other boundaries of the continuum to which it belongs as something earlier or later, but not as something with a definite distance from them.* If it is recognized, then it may not be recognized as both an earlier *and* later boundary of the continuum, but only as one of these boundaries, while it is denied that it is the other one. In the latter case we say that it is recognized in semi-plerosis and denied in semi-plerosis.[15]

15   Thus the concept of the thing is identical with the concept of the temporal itself. It includes the relative determination of something later in contrast to something earlier, and of something earlier in contrast to something later, this allows us to form the concept of something later as at a distance from something earlier, and of something earlier as at a distance from something later. If we say, this event took place 100 years ago, then this actually means: we are (that which is now is) 100 years later than this event. Thus the so-called affirmation of the event is to be understood in a manner similar to the affirmation of a thing as something that is thought, where all I actually affirm is that someone thinks this thing. After all, if someone thinks something contradictory, we can affirm that this contradiction is thought, and this so-called affirmation of something contradictory does not seem to be absurd. This is what we call an affirmation *in modo obliquo*, which obviously is not an actual affirmation of something contradictory, because we do not have a presentation of it, but of something else , *in modo recto*. If I say,

*Translators note: Reading 'solchen' for 'solchem'. p. 120.

therefore, that something existed 100 years ago, I do not actually affirm this thing; all I affirm is something real that exists 100 years later than this thing.

16   It is important to note that this being at an earlier or later distance is something very peculiar. That from which something is distant must not only be non-existent, it cannot possibly exist if that which is distant from it exists. (In the same way as I affirm that something is justifiably denied.) If something stands at varying distances from several other earlier or later things, or is earlier than one and later than another, then none of them could be thought as being compatible with the other. Thus one can say that nothing which is temporally distant from something else is compatible with it, i.e. everything from which something is distant is impossible. According to its very nature, however, one is less likely to be possible than the other one (according to its nature it would have to be thought in a more differentiated manner in order to be something that is possible, but now we are not thinking of it in terms of its specific difference). Nothing similar is encountered in other areas, e.g., distances between something coloured as coloured, something auditory as auditory, something spatial as spatial, etc. Only in those cases where the thought of temporal distance becomes connected with another thought, for example, that of spatial distance, is it possible to speak of an incompatibility between that which is distant and that from which it is distant; as, for example, I say that a thing has a local determination which differs by one mile from that which another thing had some time ago. Thus every moment in a motion is incompatible with any other moment in it. Aristotle calls this motion ἐνέργεια ἀτελής. He also calls it the actuality of a being in potentiality as such. According to our discussion, however, the latter is not true because a motion is not only no longer actually a boundary, but not even possibly one. Furthermore, what he said about motion − that it is actual only as a boundary − also applies to rest and to everything that exists, since it is a temporal process. One could say instead 'the actuality of something impossible as such'.

In the course of this temporal process, however, that which exists does not change with regard to certain specific determinations; it may even happen that it does not change with regard to any of its specific determinations except the temporal one. In relation to the latter the change is a general one and occurs only in situations where all things correspond. Thus it does not cause a difference − neither a specific one nor an individual one − between the one and the other; only in those cases where we want to speak of a difference of that which neither is nor can be, can we speak of differentiation due to a special temporal determination.[16] Thus we can say that in the actual sense we are neither dealing with specific nor with individual differences, or we can say that we are dealing with sub-individual (*unterindividuelle*) differences, by analogy with the case where nothing but temporal change occurs and where we generally speak of a complete lack of individual change.

17   That which we have said about the general concept of the thing as a boundary which forms part of a primary temporal continuum, points toward a characteristic of the first principle of all others, of that thing through which all others exist and persist. But in this case, too, existence must consist in a continual process, the direction and speed of which are completely regular, one-dimensional and immediately necessary. Yet this is the case only with regard to one of the boundaries of the process, and this boundary is distant from every other boundary as being later or earlier, as an existing boundary is distant from something non-existing or as something necessary is distant from something impossible. Many people will be surprised when they hear this, and many a theist will object at first. But that which seems absurd at first will, when we examine it closely, turn out to be the only salvation from absurdity if we believe in a changing world and in an omniscient and omnipotent creator. A creator has no co-determining cause in his works.

Furthermore, he who is omniscient knows all truth. If the truth changes, i.e. if something is true in one instance and false in another, and vice versa, then the knowledge of the omniscient being must change as well and it must change infinitesimally. The reason for this is that this being, after having recognized itself as a being earlier than a certain event, gradually and continually recognizes itself as a being coming closer and closer to this event, then existing simultaneously with it, and then recognizing itself as later and moving further and further away from it. In other words, he must recognize that the event will take place, that it will happen soon, that it is happening now and that it has happened a short time, and then a longer time, ago. What kind of God would he be if he knew the whole course of the world, but did not know what level of development it had reached? To such a God a holy penitent would be just as much sinner as saint.

NOTES

NOTES TO OSKAR KRAUS'S INTRODUCTION

1 I must point out that the term 'presentation' as Brentano used it not only refers to so-called fantasy-presentations of reproductive-presentations, but also to the so-called 'relations of consciousness' which form the very basis of judgments and emotional acts, without being themselves acts of judging or emotions.

2 In a letter which Husserl wrote to me he objects to the statement which I made in a note in the *Psychology* [p. 367 in the English edition] concerning a priority dispute between him and Meinong with regard to the Theory of Objects and Phenomenology. It was a note in his *Ideas: General Introduction to Pure Phenomenology* which caused me to make this statement [viz. Collier edition, New York and London, 1962, p. 61]. It reads as follows: 'On historical grounds I had at that time not yet dared to make use of the alienating expression Ontology, and I described their study as a fragment of an "*a priori theory of objects as such*" which A. von Meinong has brought more compactly under the title "Theory of Objects".'

I am more than willing to admit that I should not have spoken of a priority dispute between Husserl and Meinong, because my memory may have deceived me in so far as it is very possible that Meinong did not retort. I should have only spoken of a claim to priority on Husserl's part. In addition to the above quotation, such a claim is also made in the *Logical Investigations* (Vol. II, Part 1, A, 282, note 1). There Husserl calls attention to his *Philosophie der Arithmetik* which also deals with 'objects of a higher order', and expresses his regret 'that many of the more recent works on the doctrine of "Gestalt qualities" pay no attention to this work', even though rather substantial parts thereof appear, using different terminology, in treatises by Cornelius and Meinong. Husserl maintains that his work is first 'to undertake thorough research into acts and objects of a higher order'.

3 Cp. also Marty's critique in the *Untersuchungen zur Grundlegung einer allgemeinen Grammatik und Sprachphilosophie*, Halle, 1908.

4 Meinong, for example, long rejected 'emotional activities experienced as being correct' as the origin of our cognitions of value. In 1911, at the Bologna Congress he accepted them. We may assume that he succeeded in noticing something which he had previously been unable to notice. We also have an example of the reverse procedure: Russell agreed with Brentano for a long time regarding the correctness of the distinction between the state of consciousness (act) and the object of this consciousness. More recently, however, he has agreed with Mach, who does not differentiate between the fact and content (object) of the act of seeing. (Cp. Russell's *Analysis of Mind* [London and New York, 1921] and *Our Knowledge of the External World* [London and Chicago, 1914].)

5 For certain sociologists psychology is 'constructive' only in those cases where it rises above the social interaction of consciousness-endowed beings, and conjures up Hegel's 'objective spirit'.

6 If Brentano's doctrine of intensity, for example, is supposed to be 'piece-meal atomizing' (Henning) because it traces an extended grey which we see back to a field of infinitesimally small black and white dots, i.e., a mosaic of black and white, then every psychologist who looks at a mosaic from Pompeii and sees a field of coloured forms must be atomizing. Besides, according to that theory, the pattern is given only in what we see, i.e., in that which appears, and not in the appearing, i.e., the consciousness.

7 [Brentano had earlier undergone two unsuccessful eye operations, and by this time he was virtually blind from glaucoma.]

8 [I have here omitted a long section of polemical remarks by Kraus against several contemporary philosophers, Russell and Driesch in particular; others mentioned in passing are Cassirer, Jaensch, Hering, and Conrad-Martius.]

PART ONE   PRIMARY AND SECONDARY CONSCIOUSNESS
(External and Inner Perception): Perception and Apperception

I   Inner Perception (Secondary Consciousness in the Narrowest Sense)

1 This essay was meant to be the introduction to a metaphysics or theory of wisdom ('first philosophy' in the Aristotelian sense), hence it deals initially with the concept of wisdom and with epistemological questions, especially the question of direct positive insight. Since inner perception and the direct experiential knowledge connected with it constitute the basis of psychology, too, it is also very well suited to serve as an introduction to the psychology of the senses, especially since Brentano devotes a great deal of space to questions of sensory psychology here.
  The essay originally began as follows:

  1   The mere knowledge that something exists is inferior to the
  knowledge of why it exists. Hence, of those who can answer the question,
  'Why?' the one who can give not only the most immediate cause, but a
  more remote one as well, deserves the more prominent position. The

highest place, however, is reserved for the one whose knowledge extends to insight concerning the first cause which is necessary in itself. Those who achieve this are called wise, and wisdom is regarded as the most noble of the intellectual virtues.

2 Is it, then, ever possible for human beings to attain wisdom? This is frequently called into doubt; not only do people question the possibility of explaining facts by retracing them to their first causes, there are those who go so far as to deny totally both the possibility of tracing them to their more immediate causes, and also the very possibility of attaining certain factual knowledge. These are the so-called sceptics. Before we proceed to elaborate on the theory of wisdom, we will have to devote a few words to scepticism.

2 The presuppositions that Brentano speaks of here are, as will soon become apparent, nothing other than direct insights. Thus there can, in fact, be no 'presuppositionless inquiry' if we understand by that, inquiry which is not based on unproved, i.e. directly evident, truths.

On the other hand, the demand for 'presuppositionless inquiry' which Brentano himself makes elsewhere (*Die vier Phasen der Philosophie*, Leipzig, 1926, p. 173) is merely the demand for 'unprejudiced' inquiry free from partiality and preconceived ideas.

3 Prof. Alfred Kastil [1874–1951; Professor of Philosophy at Innsbruck, editor of many of Brentano's posthumously published works] comments as follows:

Even modern conventionalists are guilty of begging the question here when they teach that we cannot discover any judgement in inner perception which can be classified as direct knowledge; rather we must designate certain judgements as direct knowledge, and this happens by agreement or convention. But how could I know that other people existed and that they have come to such an agreement, if I have no direct knowledge whatsoever at my disposal? Dingler (*Zusammenbruch der Wissenschaft*, 1926) tries to obscure this issue when he suggests that we use 'discernism' or 'decreeism' rather than 'conventionalism.' But how can I know, when there is no direct knowledge, that someone has decreed something, or, that I have committed myself through such a decree to some other decree? Not even at the very moment when I do it can I directly know it, if there is no such thing as direct knowledge. Inner contradictions cannot be dispelled by means of this kind of word-play. On the other hand, Dingler would probably answer that his conventionalism does not go as far as, e.g. that of Del Negro ('Zur Evidenztheorie der Wahrheit,' *Kantstudien*, 1925), who does not allow for any directly certain factual knowledge either, while Dingler is content to deny every natural insight into universal truths. But Del Negro has, at least in this instance, consistency on his side, while Dingler, by denying all '*a priori* knowledge,' can never be sure whether, when he perceives something, he actually perceives it or not. Since conventions and decrees owe their origin only to some kind of utility, conventionalism is actually nothing but a terminological revival of pragmatism, which enjoyed great popularity a few years back.

4 Brentano calls directly evident perception direct factual cognition (*Tatsachenerkenntnis*) – Leibniz speaks of *vérités de fait*: at times Brentano speaks of factual knowledge (*Tatsachenerkenntnis*). That we must necessarily reserve the word 'knowledge' for the *vérités de raison*, as Schlick's theory of knowledge dictates, is every bit as unfounded as it would be odd to forbid Leibniz the word '*vérité*' when speaking of factual truths. 'Direct' is meant in the sense of the opposite of 'derived'.

5 Still, many epistemological theories fail to follow this the only possible path. The distinction between seeing red and seeing blue can only be made by comparing these two experiences. Only by comparison can I establish that which distinguishes between what we call 'knowing' and the so-called 'blind judgments' which are not knowledge. Cp. Kraus's Introduction and the Appendix to *Psychology From an Empirical Standpoint*. Brentano's doctrine of evidence is usually completely misunderstood. Brentano expressly warns us against believing that every evident judgment is made according to a 'criterion'. No! The evident judgment, the knowledge, is itself, as knowledge, the standard for those judgments that are not evident; it is the 'criterion' for the truth of others. In this respect Spinoza followed Descartes, and saw much more clearly than the 'modern' epistemologists that insight or knowledge is the norm for all other judgments and does not need the correspondence theory of truth for its justification.

6 In his *Third Meditation* Descartes describes his '*cogito ergo sum*' as the most important example of a clear and distinct perception.

According to Brentano every consciousness includes the perception (the evident secondary consciousness) of oneself. As we will soon see, this secondary consciousness is never distinct and is never capable of variation in terms of clarity or lack of clarity.

Thus it is certain that Cartesian direct factual knowledge goes beyond Brentano's secondary perception.

7 In other words, hearing or seeing, itself, although not a mere act of presentation, not simply an idea in the Cartesian sense, but an act of believing – a positive judgment – is not evident; it is not affirmative knowledge of the sound, i.e., I do not know the sound or the colour with evidence (but only the act of hearing a sound and of seeing a colour). The sensations (acts of sensation – states of sensation), are, however, neither cognitions nor evident acts of taking cognizance of something; nor is it possible to prove that that which we sense (that which has colour or sound – in other words, the qualitatively specified) as a matter of fact (actually, existentially) is. Nothing that it shows us *in specie specialissima* exists. At best we could say that it lets us acquire the very general concept of the qualitative-spatial and that something in actuality corresponds to this concept.

8 This is Meinong's view. The absurdity of such conjectural evidence is demonstrated by the analysis of the concept of probability. Cp. *Versuch uber die Erkenntnis*, Leipzig, 1925.

9 Obviously talk of a denial within me is not to be understood in the literal sense i.e., not in the sense of locality.

10 In the expressions 'mental activity', 'mental active being', 'mental act', the terms 'activity' and 'act' are part of the inner linguistic form and not of the meaning. In other words, one does not think of an activity; what is meant, rather, is a state of consciousness, a conscious accident of the mind.

11 The word 'real' is here, as in certain other instances, to be understood in the sense of 'actual'. 'Real', however, is a word with several meanings and can also mean 'thing', 'essence', '*res*' (in other words something that might or might not exist in actuality). This double meaning of the word is explicitly discussed in Kraus's Introduction to Brentano's *Psychology*. In the text Brentano uses this word in the sense of 'actual'.

12 Cp. *Die vier Phasen der Philosophie*, Leipzig, 1926, p. 92.

13 On the concept of probability see *Versuch über die Erkenntnis* [Leipzig, 1925].

14 The 'self-knowledge' of which Brentano speaks in this context is what he calls, in other instances, 'secondary consciousness' and what we, in order to avoid ambiguities, also call 'inner perception in the narrowest sense of the word'.

In the *Psychology* of 1874, Brentano explicitly pointed out that the hearing itself is only apprehended concomitantly in the hearing of sounds. See *Psychology*, p. 129. [References to *Psychology* are to the English edition, Routledge & Kegan Paul, 1973.]

He explains the nature of this secondary consciousness in more detail in *Psychology*, 'On Mental Reference to Something as a Secondary Object', pp. 275 ff. Here it is demonstrated that as a secondary object of mental activity, not only the reference to the primary object is to be taken into consideration, but the whole mental act which encompasses this secondary reference (the knowledge of the hearing, the consciousness of the hearing) along with the primary reference (e.g. the reference to the sound).

In secondary consciousness we can be certain that it is relatively impossible for whatever is mentally active to exist as it is while the object of the mental activity does not exist, since the mentally active being as such is identical with the object of the mentally active being, because the activity which is perceived is included in the activity of perceiving.

Thus we have established one thing: that the correctness of secondary consciousness (the impossibility of an error) is guaranteed with *a priori* evidence; it is self-evident from the nature of secondary consciousness (inner perception in the narrowest sense).

Even though some may question the evidence of this inner perception in the narrowest sense of secondary consciousness in connection with certain acts, its infallibility is beyond doubt.

15 If there is no identity between the knowing being and that which is known, we must exclude not only any direct evidence but also any possibility of direct certainty of the affirmative judgment. According to Brentano, only a directly necessary being could have it in such a case. This is a slight detour into metaphysics.

If we can prove the existence of a directly necessary being which can be regarded as the creator of all those beings (things) which are 'not necessary in themselves' (contingent) then we can prove not only the spirituality but also the perfection of this original being. According to the relevant metaphysical investigations which Brentano expounded upon in special lectures and treatises, we can also prove both that and why the act of thinking attributed to the original being (which is a part of its substance and not, like ours, merely accidental) must always comprehend the past as well as the present and the future with direct evidence. It is not possible to delve further into these questions at this point. Cp. Brentano's *Kategorienlehre*, Leipzig, 1933, and *Vom Dasein Gottes*, Leipzig, 1929.

16 Brentano here proves the statement that direct factual knowledge is only possible if the knowing being is identical with that which is known, and if this identity is simultaneously known. To this I would like to add: this identity of the knower with that which is known does not merely mean identity with regard to the mentally active subject (as would be the case with two simultaneous mental acts of the same subject) but to the identity of the subject we must add the identity of the accident, i.e., of the mental activity (the state). The mentally active being as mentally active being is identical with the object of the mentally active being; the primary and secondary mental relations which, after all, constitute the act, are conceptually different elements of the same state.

Furthermore, since Brentano is dealing here with inner perception in the narrowest sense, so-called secondary consciousness, the knowledge of the identity of the knower and the known cannot be explicit and distinct; rather, that simultaneous knowing can only be understood as an act of simultaneous perception. Consequently Brentano speaks only of a 'being known' (*'Bekanntsein'*), of a 'having knowledge' (*'Kenntnis-haben'*). As shown above, secondary consciousness refers to the entire mental state in which both the primary and the secondary references and thus also the relationship between the two is included.

The person who changes 'I think' into 'it thinks' has already missed the main point, in that he drops the identity of the subject, without which we cannot speak of an identity between the knower and that which is known.

Another question is whether the Cartesian '*cogito ergo sum*' refers only to inner perception in the narrowest sense (to the 'secondary consciousness') or whether it does not rather go beyond it and aim at an evident apperception; cp. note 6 above. The latter seems to be the case, because in no instance can a mere secondary consciousness be a *clara ac distincta perceptio*.

17 This shows that, according to Brentano, an evident perception of something transcendent would be possible only in the case where the knowing subject knew that the perception of the transcendent thing is contingent upon (e.g., caused by) that subject. It is another question whether it is possible for the same subject to have a certain perception only of the same identical activity or also of different simultaneous or temporally contiguous states of the same subject. This question will be investigated later.

18 It is obvious that Brentano is speaking here of inner perception in the

narrowest sense of the word, of the perception *en parergo* of Aristotle, i.e., of secondary consciousness. Yet the secondary consciousness is not identical with the Cartesian *cogito ergo sum*; this can only be regarded as an evident apperception, while secondary consciousness is merely an infallible – according to Brentano exclusively evident – perception. In the following investigations Brentano himself arrives at these differentiations. In my opinion, however, his interpretation of Descartes' doctrine is a bit too liberal, when he equates Descartes' 'clear and distinct comprehension' of one's own existence as a thinking being with secondary consciousness. Cp. Chapter III below.

19 Brentano discusses this doctrine in *Psychology*, Book Two, Chapter II, pp. 129 ff. One should note that Brentano speaks of secondary consciousness.

20 This plurality would not be a collective, i.e., not a group of knowing things, but a thing knowing repeatedly. Therefore, Brentano elsewhere prefers to call an act of seeing which has a spatial continuum as its object, not a continuous plurality – like its object – but rather a continuous multiplicity, in order to do justice to the unity of consciousness.

21 'Secondary consciousness' does not allow for degrees of clarity since it constitutes the act. Thus the 'direct cognitions' which Brentano speaks of here are no longer those of inner perception in the narrowest sense of the word. Their nature will be discussed in what follows. Their 'plurality' is a 'multiplicity' of qualities of the same being. 'Denial' is the term used for a judgment of the form A is not B: 'affirmation' is used for a judgment of the form A is B.

22 The negative character of all *a priori*, apodictic cognitions (of all axioms) was pointed out by Brentano, with as much clarity as anyone could want, as early as 1874. This, of course, constituted a deviation from the Aristotelian-Scholastic doctrine. Yet those very people who love to classify Brentano as a 'Scholastic' because he agrees with Aristotle on other points, and thus attempt to make him suspect to 'modern' minds, themselves adhere with indomitable stubbornness to the Aristotelian-Scholastic theory of judgment.

Galileo wrote that his contemporary Aristotelians refused, like lazy well-fed snakes, to look through the telescope, so that they would not have to see the sun-spots.

One can truly say that Brentano's contemporaries refused, with the same stubbornness, to look at the Aristotelian doctrine through Brentano's critical magnifying glass, so that they would not have to see the flaws which this doctrine exhibits in spite of all its other merits. It is true that Kant's doctrine collapses along with this Aristotelian dogma on which it is based.

23 A thorough treatment of this question is found in *Versuch über die Erkenntnis*, pp. 10 ff.

24 Concerning the concept of probability, see the appendix to *Versuch über die Erkenntnis*. On conjectural evidence see above, note 8.

25 Even today there exists a 'theory of knowledge' that refuses to see this obvious point and connects past states of consciousness with present ones through a 'unity of consciousness'.

Just as the external world is an hypothesis, although a very certain one, the identity of my present 'I' with an earlier one, whose experiences I believe myself to remember, is also an hypothesis. Yet in this case there is no direct evidence or certainty. Solipsism, too, is an assumption that can be proved to be incorrect, but must not be rejected *a priori* as nonsensical. Brentano investigates this question thoroughly in a different context. In particular, metaphysical considerations and the theistic hypothesis – at which the solipsist also may arrive – render solipsism highly improbable. The richness of the creation is incomparably greater if we assume a many-faceted world.

26 Brentano gives such a survey in the phenomenognostic sketch which follows below. As is obvious, the sketch should be made part of a metaphysical investigation and should be followed by epistemological, particularly axiomatic, propositions. The present text has not been developed to that stage; but since it dwells in particular on questions pertaining to the psychology of the senses, it is especially well-suited for this volume.

The essay, which I interrupt at this point, will be continued in Part Two, Chapter I. In between I have inserted four chapters which deal with questions connected with Part One Chapter I.

II Inner Perception in the Narrower and Broader Senses and the Possibility of Being Deceived

1 At this point I have inserted a few sections from the manuscript 'Kategorienlehre' dated 29 March 1916, into the dictation of 16 November 1915.

2 The text says 'real object' (*'reales Objekt'*). For reasons which I gave in my introduction to *Psychology From an Empirical Standpoint*, the unambiguous expression 'real thing' (*'wirkliches Ding'*), i.e. existing being, is to be preferred.

3 According to Brentano's theory, we directly comprehend, in certain cases of inner perception, an acting and being acted upon – and thus the origin of the causal concept that David Hume sought in vain. (Cp. in particular Brentano's *Versuch über die Erkenntnis* and *The Origin of Our Knowledge of Right and Wrong*, ed. Chisholm [London and New York], p. 13 n.) Thus the thinking of concepts causes in us the thinking of the axiomatic insights, and for this reason we say that they originate *ex terminis*; wanting the end constitutes the motivation for wanting the means – an experience which Schopenhauer, too, regarded as the source of the concept of causality.

In that we comprehend the effect (that which is being effected) *in modo recto*, we perceive the cause (the motivating element) of that which is being effected *in modo obliquo*; the act, however, which constitutes the motive (regardless of whether it is a conceptual presentation, wanting to achieve an end, thinking of premises, etc.) simultaneously forms (as long as it remains efficacious) part of inner perception and is at the same time directly perceived.

The motivated act exhibits the character of that which is motivated (caused) by the motivating element, and since both the causal element as well as that which is caused are inwardly comprehended (perceived) as connected, no mistake is possible as to the cause of the motivated act. Not even an omnipotent being – that is, a being that can cause every possible thing – could deceive us here by providing another cause as motive. The perception of the causal connection is a direct one in this case. If, on the other hand, a sensation is caused by something in the external world, then the causal element does not constitute part of our direct experience. Even if we take into consideration that all consciousness is, by its very nature, a suffering (an Aristotelian *passio*), and even if we were to assume that the character of such an 'affection' (cp. Kant's doctrine) is a universal quality of sensation, it would still remain completely uncertain how the sensation is caused (i.e. what the affecting thing is); we could not know whether it is a thing that is different from us or whether the cause is to be found in our own subjectivity, in our psyche itself. At best we could know that the sensation forms a necessary relation with something, that there is a 'relatively necessary connection', but we do not know with what.

'Sensation' and 'external perception' are used synonymously by Brentano.

4 I would like to stress once more that according to Brentano consciousness is always a *passio*, i.e. a being-caused, and that it is quite wrong for some critics who cannot free themselves of the 'inner linguistic form' of the word 'activity' or 'act' to criticize Brentano for regarding consciousness as an 'activity'. No! Every consciousness is a *passio*, a suffering in the Aristotelian sense of the word, because it is a being-acted-upon. Obviously, however, this does not exclude the possibility that consciousness itself can cause something else. And this applies to the act of willing as well, a fact that is often misunderstood by others. The willing being is also someone who is acted upon and thus someone who is determined. This does not rule out his simultaneously causing something, and, in particular, his causing the object of his act of will, his so-called 'end'. Not only is 'freedom of will' in the sense of 'power of the will' compatible with the fact that the act of will is determined, without it it would be non-existent, especially in reference to the human will, because without it our will would not have the power to bring about or to halt future decisions of our will. Cp. *Origin of Our Knowledge of Right and Wrong*, ed. Chisholm [London and New York, 1969].

5 It is generally believed that the sensation of the sensed object, i.e. of that which we sense as object, is caused. We believe that we see yellow or blue things because the things that we see actually are blue or yellow, and blue and yellow things cause our seeing, although somewhat careful deliberation will show that this assumption is incorrect.

6 Concerning the theory of the perception of time, cp. the Appendix to *Psychology From an Empirical Standpoint*, and Oskar Kraus's *Franz Brentano: Zur Kenntnis seines Lebens und seiner Lehre*, Munich, 1919,

pp. 39 ff as well as Chapter V below and Part Two, Chapter III. See also Franz Brentano, 'Raum and Zeit', *Kantstudien*, Vol. XXV (1920, pp. 1–23).

7 Some psychologists actually believe that each remembrance of previous experiences is a kind of weaker repetition of these past acts. Brentano points out, on the contrary, that mental acts are not merely secondary objects of our presentations and judgments but primary ones as well. I can imagine my previous pain as I would imagine an external object in my fantasy; I can think of it in the same way as I would think of an external object by making it my primary object.

When I believe that I have experienced something or when I expect a future experience, I do not perceive it in an inner perceptual way but rather I have a presentation of it as I would have a presentation of something physical, i.e. I make it into my primary object.

If a mistake that I once committed is now made my primary object, I do not have to 'experience' it a second time. This shows at the same time how ineptly some people express themselves when they speak of 'experiencing' the primary object, e.g. colours, sounds, or things in general that we have presentations of.

8 Apperceptions, although they do not belong to inner perception in the strict sense, can nevertheless be evident, as is shown in Chapter III.

9 The theory that inner perception (secondary consciousness) is always evident is contested for other reasons as well. But none of the considerations that give rise to these objections leads to the denial of the invariable correctness of the secondary consciousness which, as shown above, is established *a priori*.

10 See Brentano, 'Uben ein optisches Paradoxon', *Zeitschrift für Psychologie und Physiologie der Sinnesorgane* (Vol. 3, 1892 and Vol. 5, 1893), and 'Zur Lehre von den optischen Täuschugen', *Zeitschrift für Psychologie und Physiologie der Sinnesorgane* (Vol. 4, 1894).

11 Cp. note 22 to Chapter I. Cp. also Marty's *Untersuchungen zur Grundlegung einer allgemeinen Grammatik*, etc., Halle, 1918, as well as his *Gesammelte Schriften* [Halle, 1916–20, 2 vols]. If we consider propositions of the form, 'the sum of the angles of all triangles is equivalent to 2 right angles' to be affirmative, what we do, in fact, is to think something negative: we apodictically deny that any triangle can have 2 right angles. Yet having been misled by the language, we still believe ourselves to be judging positively. The secondary consciousness that comprehends the negative denial does not deceive us, but we make the wrong judgment concerning our negative judgment (and concerning the secondary consciousness implied in it), by making it the object of our primary consciousness.

12 Some psychologists equate sensory pleasure and sensory pain as 'so-called sensations of feeling' ('*sogenannte Gefuhlsempfindungen*') with sensory qualities. But just as colours and sounds can be the objects of belief – but of unjustified belief, if this doctrine were correct, we would not 'perceive' our pains and pleasures, but would at best merely believe that we have them, and we could be deceived as to whether or not they really exist!

13 Sensory pleasure and sensory pain are emotional affects, i.e. an intense hatred or an intense love (pleasantness or unpleasantness of certain

sensations). One sensory sensation is pleasant, another one unpleasant to me, and the pleasantness or unpleasantness has the intensity of the sensation to which it relates. It is quite wrong to speak here of a consciousness of a state, which consciousness lacks 'intentionality', i.e. directedness towards something, and thus could not be called 'object consciousness'. For it is not at all difficult to show what the object of that emotional consciousness is. What is unpleasant about sensory displeasure is the sensory sensation itself, i.e. the sensing of this or that quality is painful to me; I hate it intensely, indeed, with the intensity of that sensation itself. This applies, *mutatis mutandis*, to the analogues of sensory pleasure. Sensory pleasure and sensory pain, which Brentano counts as affects, do then have to do with 'intentions', namely with those whose object is the sensing of certain qualities. In these cases we encounter secondary consciousness not only in the sense of believing in the sensory act, but also in the sense of a love or hatred towards this act.

14 In the case of affects, the love or hate is directed strictly towards the sensing of the quality, i.e. towards me as a sensing being, and not towards the quality itself, except indirectly; sensing something bitter is unpleasant to me, sensing something sweet may be pleasant or unpleasant to me.

Brentano notes that it is difficult here to prove that there is an appearance of qualities at all; those who speak here merely of consciousness of a state and do not see a consciousness of an object, obviously miss the object of the sensation that is unpleasant to us, i.e. they are unable to detect it and cannot differentiate it from the affect.

It is even stranger that others, quite to the contrary, are unable to detect the affective nature, i.e. the emotional character, of sensory pleasure and pain, and treat these emotional activities as though they were mere qualities, that is, like the objects of our colour or sound sensations. Another one of Husserl's errors that goes even further and also denies the intentional character of non-emotional sensory sensations, is discussed in the introduction to *Psychology From An Empirical Standpoint*.

Whoever denies that every consciousness is a consciousness of something and whoever says that sensations or affects lack this characteristic, abandons the most elementary knowledge of psychology just as much as a person who teaches that presentation, judgment or emotion lack secondary consciousness.

15 This theory is thoroughly discussed in the *Untersuchungen zur Sinnespsychologie*, Leipzig, 1907.

16 Sensory pleasure and displeasure that are connected with seeing or hearing are not included in the visual or auditory sensation, but rather other 'feeling sensations' ('*Spürempfindungen*') are set off by the visual or auditory sensations and accompany them and are confounded with them. These affects, pleasure and displeasure, are not so much brought about by isolated sensations as by sensation-complexes (either simultaneous or successive).

17 Marty considered the concept of the effective cause to be a synthetic one. Cp. his *Raum and Zeit*, Halle, 1915.

Brentano, on the other hand, finds the archetype of this concept in various cases of inner perception, from which it is acquired by means of simple abstraction: in the various acts of motivation, in the derivation of axiomatic insights from the concepts, etc. Cp. *The Origin of Our Knowledge of Right and Wrong* [London and New York, 1969], and note 3 above.

18 Brentano answers the questions set forth here as follows: Every mental activity (every consciousness) relates to something which becomes its object (cp. note 12); the relationship is a many-faceted one (cp. *Psychology From An Empirical Standpoint*); the differences between present, past and future are comprehended by us in connection with those between the temporal modes (cp. *Psychology*, Appendix, and further comments below, as well as note 6).

Only the sensations and affects possess intensity. Conditions other than sensations and affects have no intensity. 'Intensity' in the sense of the density of the appearance in the sensory field is applicable synonymously to all kinds of senses. Besides that, there can be one other sense of 'intensity', as in those cases where we are dealing with different kinds of qualities which may exhibit something like a different efficacy (forcefulness). ... Each sensation is localized in some way according to its 'object', i.e. each quality appears to us somehow in a spatial dimension, and that which appears spatially to us can indeed be called spatial in fully the same sense of the term. It is quite erroneous to speak of an inhomogeneity of tactile, optical, etc. spaces. Each of them allows us to acquire the concept of something spatially extended in the same sense of the word. Additional details about this question are to be found at various places in this volume; cp., for instance, note 8 to Part One, Chapter I. According to Brentano we will find the presentation of a substance included in inner and external experience, provided we regard ourselves as thinking beings with regard to the former, and provided we intuit something suitably extended in the latter case. The intuition of effect and cause is given repeatedly in inner perception. (Cp. the preceding note.)

19 This paragraph is taken from a discussion of sufficient reason dated 10 January 1917.

20 As in Chapter I, Section 1, Brentano here characterizes the difference between evident and blind judgments by saying that blind judgments are the results of blind impulses. This, however, is a genetic characteristic, not a descriptive or phenomenal one (or, as some prefer to say nowadays, 'phenomenological').

The question remains then, how are we to characterize the difference which appears when we compare so-called evident judgments with so-called blind judgments? Should we say: blind judgments lack evidence, are void of evidence? Does the blind, accidentally correct judgment remain exactly what it is, except that it has become an evident one? Is evidence a quality which can be added on or taken away?

One objection to such a view is that it has the peculiar result that an evident judgment would come into being simply by adding evidence to a blind judgment; in other words, the evident judgment would include a blind judgment. ...

21 The term 'measure' here refers to an inexact measuring, i.e. a mere estimation, an evaluative comparison.

22 In other words, he believes that he is seeing the direction of the line other than he is in fact seeing it; this belief, which he recognizes as such, he considers erroneously to be something that is determined in the process of seeing the line. Yet the seeing of the line does not show him this direction and the inner perception of the act of seeing (the secondary consciousness of seeing, which is given together with this act) does not perceive the act of seeing as seeing this other direction. The visual phenomenon remains unchanged, but we are led to believe that it has changed, as in certain so-called illusions of perspective or with the Aristotelian ball trick [See p. 13]. And it is no less surprising that the resulting (though incorrect) findings of a comparison are believed to be part of the compared phenomena than it is that pain affects are believed to be localized.

23 Many characterologists not only make this mistake, but go even further and believe they have direct knowledge of other people's character traits. Something is attributed to intuition and '*Wesensschau*' which belongs, at best, to the realm of instinct, behaviour, or the like, for example the correct comprehension of the expressive movements in and between animals. To my knowledge Husserl has never gone that far with his '*Wesensschau*'.

24 In my opinion the word 'usually' should be inserted here.

25 Here Brentano is saying that whoever would count sensory pleasure and pain as sensory qualities such as sounds or colours would have to maintain that these are cases of directly certain external perception, because we comprehend pleasure and pain with direct certainty. If, however, an advocate of this doctrine admits that external perception is never directly certain, then he would have to regard himself as justified in doubting the existence of his pain or his pleasure. (Cp. notes 14 and 17 above.)

III   A More Detailed Discussion of Perceiving, Comparing and Differentiating
(*An Essay on Descartes*' 'clare ac distincte percipere')

1 I have here inserted a discussion from an essay entitled 'Metaphysics' dated 23 May 1916. It gives us an idea of the persistence with which Brentano pursued the investigation of these problems even at an advanced age.

   He comes to the conclusion that acts of comparing, differentiating, and apperceiving differ from what he calls 'inner perception' ('secondary consciousness'), and that these apperceptive activities can be evident.

2 A more thorough analysis of the ontological argument is contained in Brentano's essay entitled 'Über Kants Kritik der Gottesbeweise' in *Die vier Phasen der Philosophie*, Leipzig, 1926, pp. 83–7. Cp. also Anton Marty, *Untersuchungen zur Grundlegung der allgemeinen Grammatik und Sprachphilosophie*, Halle, 1908, pp. 346 ff. Those assertions which, according to Descartes, predicate of a thing something that is contained in its very concept, are apodictic, negative cognitions that spring from the concepts (are evident *ex terminis*). Cp. Oskar Kraus's essay on Spinoza in *Euphorion* (1927).

3 Cp. Chapter I, section 12 above. The statement used by Brentano comes from Descartes' *De Principii*, section 46. The example is as follows: In the

case of a so-called toothache or some other pain that is localized in a part of the body, we are dealing with an instance of the sense of feeling (*des Spürsinnes*) mentioned in Chapter II, (see especially note 19 thereto), i.e. an unpleasant or painful sensing of certain feelings. These feelings, like all sensory qualities are phenomenally localized in some way. That means I originally sense them somewhere, yet their localization is very indeterminate. This localization, however, is phenomenal; I sense a quality as existing somewhere, but my act of sensing has no localization and is not perceived as existing somewhere. The same holds true of the pain with which I feel my act of sensing, i.e. the painful sensation, the affect of pain.

Since the object of the sensation (which is painful to us) appears to be localized, we also localize the act itself, because we confuse act and object. We carry our error even further by believing that the pain is located at that point where the peripheral cause of our pain is located in our (transcendentally existing) body, e.g. in the tooth or the leg.

This error may serve a biological purpose, but nevertheless it is an error based on a confusion.

4 The statement that 'eternal truths' exist only 'in the mind' is a phrase which Brentano took from Aristotle, and it is explained in detail in Kraus's Introduction to *Psychology From an Empirical Standpoint*, and by Brentano in the Appendix to that work.

If someone, for example, thinks of an 'eternal truth' of mathematics, for example the theorem about the sum of the angles of a triangle, this thought amounts to knowledge, indeed to negative apodictic knowledge which gives him the insight that a triangle, the sum of whose angles does not add up to two right angles, is impossible. He may also know that knowledge of the opposite is utterly impossible. In other words, a person can never arrive at a correct judgment if he judges in the opposite manner. Yet it would be a serious mistake to believe of the theorem concerning the sum of the angles of a triangle, that somewhere, in an eternal realm of immutable truths, it exists, subsists, or has any other mystical form of being. This knowledge, which Brentano arrived at during his later years (it was published in 1911 but had been advocated in letters long before) is our salvation. It is based on psychological investigations and a critique of language that put an end to errors that go back as far as Plato. It is knowledge which itself should be counted among the 'eternal truths' in the above-mentioned sense.

5 This means: their axiomatic character is destroyed by the assumption that God has power over them.

6 Cp. above, Chapter I, section 10.

7 I.e. '*quod clare ac distincte percipio verum est*'.

8 In order clearly to express the character of an axiom in linguistic terms, i.e. the character of negative apodictic cognition, the sentence, 'An evident judgment is true', should run, 'An evident judgment which is not true is impossible'. Since 'true', however, means 'cannot possibly contradict an evident judgment' we clearly see the contradictory nature of the sentence. ('Contradictory' means diametrically opposed judgments about the same matter.) Knowledge that contradicts knowledge (i.e. knowledge that is in error) is impossible.

9 Attention is not consciousness. Rather, it is a sometimes arbitrarily produced condition of the mental subject that facilitates the act of noticing.

10 Cp. note 3 to Chapter III above.

11 Inner perception in the sense of secondary consciousness contains no deception; it cannot make comparisons and consequently cannot confuse anything. In so far as it does not make any distinctions Brentano calls it 'confused', 'implicit', 'indistinct'. For this very reason, however, Brentano's secondary consciousness cannot be identical with Descartes' '*cogito, ergo sum*' because Descartes calls the perception of the thinking being a *clara ac distincta percipio*. In Brentano, however, a *clara ac distincta percipio* is given only in explicit, distinct perceiving, i.e. noticing or apperceiving.

Descartes himself, however, does not clearly distinguish between inner perception in the sense of secondary consciousness and inner perception in the sense of distinct and explicit evident noticing. Neither does he make a clear distinction between this evident noticing and *a priori* cognitions.

12 The mental state that is called 'attention' is sometimes produced involuntarily by certain elements of consciousness, and sometimes it is voluntarily brought about. In the latter case we sometimes encounter a higher and sometimes a lesser degree of so-called effort of will. The state of attention, of heightened and intensified readiness to receive impressions, is not itself consciousness, but is caused and accompanied by acts of consciousness.

13 Cp. *The Origin of Our Knowledge of Right and Wrong*, London and New York, 1969.

14 'To compare something with something else' means to direct one's attention towards one thing or the other and to take note of differences, e.g. of size, or common traits (conformities). Cp. *Psychology*, Introduction.

15 For example, I now hear a sequence of two tones; later I recall that I heard this sequence of tones. I thus make my previous act of hearing this sequence of tones a primary object, although it was originally a secondary object, i.e. an object of inner perception in the narrowest sense of the word. Now, via recollection, I have a primary presentation of both my previous act of hearing and the originally secondary consciousness; I employ the same *modus rectus* of the present and the same *modus obliquus* of the past which my act of hearing originally had.

The 'temporal modes of the present and the recent past' that accompany every sensation of something are presented along with the memory of the sensation.

16 Comparisons of consecutive temporal happenings in memory – although they may be separated by temporal intervals – are possible, but deceptions in memory may occur.

Aside from these deceptions in memory, the fact that the things remembered have different temporal locations does not impede the comparison, because the things remembered always appear with the same temporal modes of the present and recent past as the original act. Here we have an advantage over spatial comparisons in which distant things, i.e. spatially different things, are compared, because the spatial distance does impede the comparison, even in those cases where the spatially distant things are given at the same time.

Temporally distant events appear in memory, however, with the same temporal modes, so that the difference in temporal location can only be effective as the cause of deceptions of memory.

17 This seems to mean: if the same linguistic expressions are used for the subject of the negation.

18 In other words, the knowledge of comparative determinations (*komparative Bestimmungen, Vergleichsbestimmungen*) is not a matter of inner perception in the narrowest sense of the word (not a matter of secondary consciousness), even though relations (*Relatives*) of various kinds are inwardly given in the perceiving being as objects of consciousness.

19 Cp. note 39 to Part Two, Chapter I.

20 Cp. *Psychology*, and Chapter III, note 8 above. 'False' means something that cannot possibly be evident. Something that cannot possibly be in accordance with knowledge.

IV   Summary and Supplementary Remarks on Perceiving and Noticing (Perception and Apperception)

1 This summary is taken from various essays and dictations: section 1 from an essay dated 24 June 1914; section 2 from an essay entitled 'Selbstbewußtsein' which is undated but comes from the last decade of Brentano's life; the note pertaining to section 2 is taken from a letter that has already been published in Kraus's Introduction to *Psychology From an Empirical Standpoint*; section 3 comes from notes taken by Anton Marty in Schönbühel, date unknown; section 4 has been culled from a dictation taken down by Oskar Kraus in Schönbühel in 1901.

At that time Brentano had written a 'psychognostic sketch'. As we went over it together, he made these remarks which struck me even then as being of great importance. In his later sketches nothing similar has been found so far. It is possible, however, that similar remarks might be found in older manuscripts or in his abundant correspondence with psychologists.

The concluding sections are taken from a 'Kategorienlehre' of 2 February 1916.

2 I distinguish so-called 'logical parts' with regard to one and the same thinking thing if I, as judging or loving being, explicitly recognize in myself the 'mentally active being'; this, however, is a wholly inappropriate use of the term 'part' and it would be better to abandon it.

I distinguish accidentally connected parts if I distinguish in myself, as a mentally active being, the seeing and hearing being.

3 These cognitions can be called direct factual knowledge, in contrast to conclusions, which constitute indirect knowledge. For in the former no premises are given from which inferences are drawn. Yet these cognitions by no means constitute direct inner perception, as does secondary consciousness. Brentano made this clear in Chapter III, section 4 above; the following remarks elucidate the same point.

4 In his *Erkenntnislehre*, Moritz Schlick does not want to admit that we sometimes experience a chord distinctly and sometimes indistinctly while still experiencing it as the same chord. A person may hear C, E, G without distinguishing the hearing of the individual notes; another time he may hear each note separately. Schlick says in his epistemology that the chord experienced, this directly experienced auditory image, 'is a different thing in either case'. Unfortunately we do not learn whether Schlick believes that we hear different notes, i.e. that we no longer hear C, E, G at all, or why this chord is nevertheless designated as one and the same. It is certainly correct that the experiences are different in the two cases mentioned, for the simple reason that one is an experience of noticing, the other of distinguishing ('noticing' alone is not enough; we must also differentiate between the things noticed.) Cp. below Part Two, Chapter I.

5 Brentano remarks correctly in his *Psychology* of 1874 that inner perception can never become inner observation. Yet he went too far when he said that there is no inner observation that can be distinguished from inner perception. Cp. *Psychology*, Introduction, Section VIII.

6 This note is taken from a letter to Carl Stumpf.

7 If it could appear as secondary consciousness – which is impossible – then the apperceiving act would be a part of one and the same act as the apperceived act.

8 We see that this concept of apperception has nothing to do with the term as used in reference to a transcendent interpretation of the thing perceived and a further elaboration thereof.

Apperception is used here in the strict and narrow sense of explicit, evident noticing.

9 The mental substance is the mental subject. The mental subject, when perceiving itself as a mentally active (conscious) being, perceives itself, but only in general terms, neither as an individual nor as a physical or mental individual. As pointed out before, it is only *a priori* self-evident that the perceiving being cannot be identical with two subjects.

The perceptions that are mentioned in the text are not direct inner perceptions in the sense of secondary consciousness, but evident apperceptions. They constitute direct evident knowledge in so far as they are not inferred.

10 In my opinion this is to be understood as follows: I can comprehend my act of seeing in secondary consciousness and I can perceive my simultaneous act of hearing in a secondary perception that is a part thereof. In each case the subject (the 'I') is implied in general. A third perception, an evident act of noticing, can now include both these evident perceptions, i.e. I can notice that I hear and that I see. If now my act of seeing, together with the secondary consciousness that perceives it, is absent, then naturally the noticing which encompasses both conditions is also absent. Whereas the remaining mental state, together with its secondary consciousness, remains unchanged, and can continue to be noticed.

Brentano adds: this comprehensive perception is to be understood as a distinct one, i.e. as an act of noticing, which is connected with a differentiation between the two perceptions (the acts of seeing and hearing).

Yet it is also possible that the wider perception remains as an act of noticing the acts of seeing and hearing without differentiating explicitly between hearing and seeing. He calls such non-differentiating and non-comparing noticing of two conditions 'confused'.

11 This paragraph supplements the former as well as the doctrine of secondary consciousness in general.

I hear and I see. The secondary consciousness of myself as a hearing being differs from my secondary consciousness of myself as a seeing being. Naturally it also differs from the secondary consciousness of the being that compares both states. Nevertheless we can have all three secondary 'consciousnesses' simultaneously; in the absence of the act of seeing, obviously only the secondary consciousness pertaining to the act of hearing remains. We can also continue to hear and to see. Then obviously the secondary consciousness pertaining to each of these acts remains, while it is not necessary for us to continue to compare these two conditions as such or even to notice them. To use the term 'unconscious' in this context would be wrong.

12 I.e. I merely have a memory presentation of my earlier act of seeing and thereby make it my primary object.

V   *Perception* in modo recto, modo obliquo *and the Perception of Time*

1 The original title of this chapter was 'Zur Lehre von der Empfindung', dated 26 December 1914.

2 This would apply to all those who teach that there exists a presenting, judging, emotionally active being, who has no secondary consciousness of this activity.

3 In this context Brentano used the phrase, 'sense ... as sensing beings'. This phrase clearly expresses the fact that secondary consciousness cannot be separated from primary consciousness. Yet it would not be a good idea to apply this linguistic formulation analogously to all cases of secondary consciousness.

4 As beings who are conscious of our sensation (in inner perception), we are directly conscious of the sensation, and indirectly conscious, i.e. *in modo obliquo*, of that which is sensed.

As beings who have a sensation of something, we are primarily and directly focused on that which we sense (on the object of the sensation).

5 Brentano wrote, 'phenomenal affirmation'. I have altered the text to clarify the meaning.

6 In this context 'object' means, as it so often does, 'thing'.

7 We must add here 'of the same object'.

8 I understand this as follows: I look at myself, i.e. at my states of consciousness, with inner perception (as secondary object) *in modo recto* in the *modus praesens* (the mode of the present). At the same time, however, I perceive myself, ἐν παρέργῳ as a being that perceives indirectly (*modo obliquo*), something other than itself, namely, the so-called 'primary objects', e.g. coloured things, sounding things, etc.

That is to say, as a sensing being I have a presentation of 'the primary objects' *in modo recto* and believe in them, yet as an inwardly perceiving being I perceive them indirectly. This perception of primary objects *in modo obliquo* varies from the *modus praesentis* to a series of limited, contiguous modes of the past. Thus, speaking from the point of view of inner perception, I perceive myself as a being that perceives primary objects indirectly (*modo obliquo*). One of these modes is the *modus praesentis*, the others are preterite modes. These modes are simultaneously present to us.

The intuition of the duration of physical objects is based on the fact that I sense the object with a simultaneously given temporal *modus continuum*, that comes into being successively and changes successively. Regarding the intuition of motion each one of the temporally contiguous boundary modes relates to determinations of place which differ from each other infinitesimally.

It is interesting to note that the *modus praesentis* of external perception (e.g. when hearing a melody, when seeing a motion) is called a *modus obliquus*, but this is only as seen from the standpoint of inner perception. Because with inner perception the sensing being, not that which is sensed, e.g. not the sound, not the colour, etc., is the direct object. In most cases, however, Brentano simply calls the present mode the *modus rectus*, thereby referring both to the mode with which I now hear the note C, as well as to the mode in which I perceive myself as so hearing.

From the standpoint of the sensing being as such, the *modus praesentis* is in fact just as directly focused on the primary object as secondary perception is focused on the primary consciousness and on itself.

Continually changing temporal modes of sensation are the sole means through which we can experience the succession and duration of external objects. In perceiving this continuum of modes, we sense, for example, a note that has not altered in intensity or quality as 'just now past', as 'having existed earlier and earlier'. Cp. Part One, Chapter V, section 10, and Part Two, Chapters II and III.

There is another point which I would like to stress. Many psychologists confuse the knowledge that everything that is must exist for a certain time, i.e. must last for a certain length of time, with the erroneous if not absurd opinion that the temporal continuum has more than one actual boundary point, i.e. that there actually exists more than one precise present point. Naturally every sensation lasts for a certain period of time, and this naturally also holds true for proteraesthesis and its inner perception. Nevertheless, however, we perceive ourselves inwardly (continuously) at every moment as a temporal boundary, and, yet, in proteraesthesis, the *modus praesentis* is still a boundary mode.

9 Much of what the Gestalt theorists, who are adverse to analysis, ascribe to a 'configuration of sound' ('*Tongestalt*'), is to be explained in the manner indicated in the text. Cp. Brentano's *Untersuchungen zur Sinnespsychologie*, Leipzig, 1907.

10 Marty set forth such a theory in his posthumous book, *Raum und Zeit*, Halle, 1915.

11 The question is how we arrive at presentations of the future. Brentano

suggests two possibilities: (1) that we attain it somehow or other directly in the form of an expectation or the like, or (2) that, by means of the intuition of the distance between something later and something earlier (which we find in the so-called intuition of the past), we attain the possibility of considering the present as something earlier in contrast to something later. Brentano adopts this second possibility.

12 I remember a previous experience, thereby making the experience a primary object; the temporal mode which emerges can hardly be differentiated from the present mode. Soon, however, corrective judgments appear, which introduce approximate time-measuring determinants, and reveal that the *modus praesentis* cannot be applied in this case.

13 In my opinion, Brentano maintains that the only tenable view is the old conception according to which secondary consciousness accompanies primary consciousness without exception; that we, as sensing beings, have something as object *in modo recto*, while, at the same time, perceiving ourselves as sensing beings *in modo recto*. Furthermore it states that we also present *in modo obliquo*, that which we have as external object, i.e. we present it from the point of view of secondary consciousness, and from the point of view of primary consciousness we consider it to be true and believe in it. This section number 11 was added as a later revision.

14 Husserl made this mistake. I would rather doubt the evidence of inner perception in certain instances than ever to ascribe evidence to external perception. Even if inner perception is not always insightful, it is never deceptive (cp. p. 94), while so-called external perception, i.e. sensation, can never be proved to be logically justified.

15 Kant, too, is guilty of this. Cp. here Brentano, *Die vier Phasen der Philosophie*, Leipzig, 1926, pp. 92 ff and 162.

16 Brentano added another note at this point, which refers once more to the question of whether it would not after all be possible, that we only sense ourselves, i.e. that we have only ourselves as direct objects – like Aristotle's God, who has nothing but himself, as knowing being, as direct object.

The phrase 'that we, when sensing ourselves, have ourselves as direct objects' is a rather unfortunate formulation. We do not sense ourselves, rather we directly perceive our act of sensing. Cp. section 9.

The question should therefore be formulated as follows: do we only have our act of sensing (our sensing activity), our state of sensation, as direct object of our inner perception – just as God, according to Aristotle, has nothing but himself as knowing being as direct object of knowledge?

This question, whether we directly perceive our sensing and whether we only indirectly perceive that which we sense (the so-called primary object) must be answered affirmatively. Consequently what Brentano appends is still correct:

> Strictly speaking, then, we would not be dealing with a double
> perception, but with a unitary one, the self-perception, the inner
> perception, which allows us, at the same time, to present external objects
> *in modo obliquo* as our phenomena, and therefore, *in modo obliquo*.

Yes, indeed! From the standpoint of inner perception, that which we, as sensing beings, have as direct object is perceived only indirectly *in modo obliquo*. Thus we actually affirm it no more than we affirm the existence of ghosts when we affirm the evidence of someone who believes in ghosts.

When we affirm ourselves with evidence as beings who sense colours, we do not thereby affirm the colours with evidence.

Brentano continues, 'This would give us a new reason for rejecting as utterly impossible the view that we also have unconscious external perceptions'. This conclusion, too, is justified. So-called 'external perception' bears this name quite illegitimately; it is a mere blind belief in that which we sense. We are only certain of the existence of this blind belief in sensory qualities, however, through inner perception in the sense of secondary consciousness; indeed, it is only made possible through secondary consciousness, as is illustrated below and in *Psychology from an Empirical Standpoint*, cp. esp. p. 329. In the *Psychology* Brentano states (p. 92), 'mental phenomena are those phenomena which alone can be perceived in the strict sense of the word'. 'This definition, too, is an adequate characterization of mental phenomena'. Originally Brentano described 'the intentional (or mental) inexistence of the object' as 'that feature which best characterizes' mental phenomena. Later, however, realizing that the doctrine of immanence is false, he came to see the reference to inner perception and to the relation of inner perception to primary consciousness as being of equal significance.

Brentano's doctrine is that my consciousness is specifically differentiated, on the one hand, by means of its various modes (presentations, judgments, emotions) as well as direct and indirect modes, and, on the other hand, by differences in the objects of consciousness.

If at one time I think of Pegasus and at another time of Cerberus, neither one of them exists. The question was then raised how my consciousness can be changed by something which does not exist and which, according to Brentano, does not have mental or intentional existence either. After all, an actual relation in the sense of an actual connection is not present!

The following answer has been given to this question:

No primary consciousness is possible without secondary consciousness. Secondary consciousness is directed toward primary consciousness and toward the entire act. On the one hand, I perceive myself as a being thinking of Pegasus and as the perceiving being which is thinking in this way; on the other hand I perceive myself as a being that is thinking of Cerberus and as the perceiving being thinking in this way. Thus we are dealing with a differentiation of the perceiving being by means of something that actually is, and that he himself actually is. Now comes the important point. We must not say that the differentiation is brought about by something which is in no way the perceiving being, and to which this being has no connection. This seems to be the case, e.g. if we allow for a differentiation of mental states by means of the object of the act of thinking of the mentally active being, when this object is not identical with this being.

Besides, the method employed to grasp the ultimate differences in consciousness must be the same as the method which enables us to recognize differences among things given (among so-called objects): the comparative method. This is how I recognize that my act of seeing something red is generically different from the red that I see; that I see something specifically different when I see something red and when I see something blue; and again that I apperceive with evidence something specifically different when I notice my act of seeing red than when I notice my act of seeing blue.

17 This essay (section 12) is entitled 'Von der Zeit', date unknown, but certainly post 1906 and most likely post 1911 (i.e. after the publication of *Die Klassifikation der Psychischen Phänomene*). It presumably dates from 1914.

18 I.e. we can no longer predicate of it that it is red. (Brentano assumes here the existence of colours.)

19 This would be a case of heterogeneity because an existing thing, e.g. a present king, and a past thing, e.g. a former king would not fall under the same concepts if the temporal change were a change in objects.

20 A note C, which I sense as just past, falls under the same concept as the note C when I sensed it as present.

21 Cp. the elaboration on this phrase: 'reference to an object' in the *Psychology*. According to Brentano himself it would be better to say, 'every mental state of consciousness is a reference to something'.

22 This note is taken from a letter Brentano wrote to Marty on 10 March 1906.

23 Cp. *Psychology*, pp. 328–9. This explanation does not solve the time problem. Nevertheless, the present investigations clearly point a way towards answering this extremely difficult question. Cp. *Psychology*, Appendix.

PART TWO   PHENOMENOGNOSY OF SENSORY AND NOETIC CONSCIOUSNESS

I   A Survey of so-called Sensory and Noetic Objects of Inner Perception

1 The following sketch is the continuation of Chapter I, paragraph 16, in the manuscript; there it was numbered 18 but I included the first two paragraphs in the notes to Part One, Chapter I.

2 Some Gestalt theorists speak rather derogatorily of any psychology which teaches that mental states (acts) are composed of elements. Such a critique in fact reveals a misunderstanding of the most elementary aspects of psychological research and a naive superstition that every element must form part of a collective whole (a 'sum'). Cp. *Psychology From an Empirical Standpoint*, p. 290 n and the Introduction.

3 These lines, too, reveal that the expression 'something mentally active' is simply synonymous with the expression 'thinking thing' (the Cartesian *cogitans*).

4 It is important to note that the statement runs as follows: he who sees something, he who hears something, the mentally active being in general refers to something. This something is 'that, which it has as its object'.

Instead of saying 'to refer to something' one can also say 'to have something as object'. It is completely wrong to maintain that the mental relation is directed towards an 'intentional object in the sense of an immanent object', which is to be understood as the correlate of the act or the relation. What led to this utterly mistaken doctrine is the mode of expression Brentano previously used in connection with older doctrines, 'no act of seeing without something that is seen, no act of hearing without something that is heard'; and this phrase made it appear as though in the 'intentional relation to something' a correlate is given. Brentano, however, has long been aware that this is a mistake and he sets matters right in a detailed way in the Appendix to *Psychology From an Empirical Standpoint*. It is also regrettable that the expression 'intention', which has nothing to do with an emotional intention, and which simply means 'direction towards something' has given rise to the distinction between 'fulfilled and unfulfilled intentions'! Anton Marty, in his *Untersuchungen zur Grundlegung der allegemeinen Grammatik und Sprachphilosophie* (Halle, 1908) pointed out this misunderstanding; so did Brentano in the Appendix to his *Psychology*. In my introduction to Brentano's *Psychology* I pointed out that this doctrine could be based only on an inadequate differentiation between so-called 'external perception' in the narrower sense and external perception in the broader sense; in the latter, external perception is to be understood as conceptual and transcendent interpretation of that which is sensed (*begriffliche und transscendente Deutung des Empfundenen*).

5 In the text the term 'sensed' is used. Yet the expression 'to sense oneself as one who sees' is not a very happy way of describing the fact of the self-perception of the sensing being. Secondary consciousness, after all, accompanies every other mental activity, too, e.g. axiomatic knowledge. Cp. Part One, Chapter V.

6 If I deny something or desire something, then I must, at the same time, have a presentation of this thing. Thus the judgmental relation and the emotional relation in some way include a presentational relation. For this reason Brentano felt justified in speaking of a double relation. The relation of the presentation included in the judgment or the emotion to the act concerned, however, still requires further explanation. Brentano says that the judgment and the emotion 'presuppose' presenting.

7 Brentano's theory of judgment is explained in *Psychology*, Book Two. Neither Hillebrand's (*Die neuen Theorien der kategorischen Schlusse*, Vienna, 1891) nor Marty's (cp. his *Gesammelte Schriften*, Halle, 1916–20) defence of Brentano's doctrine has succeeded as yet in overcoming the Aristotelian-Scholastic theory of judgment.

Some critics choose to reject Brentano as a 'Scholastic' because there are a number of important points in which he does agree with Aristotle; these critics, on the other hand, bow to the authority of the Stagirite and his Scholastic followers precisely in those cases where Brentano has proved the Aristotelian point of view to be untenable.

8 All the so-called axioms, the Law of Contradiction, causal laws and all true 'laws' deny something as impossible. Assuming the correctness of the Law of Inertia, when we state it, we are denying that a body can ever change its

state of rest or its uniform linear motion without some external cause. In mathematics we say that it is impossible for one unit added to another unit to result in anything but two; or that the sum of the angles of a triangle could amount to anything other than two right angles. (Kant, for example, and some of his Scholastic predecessors such as Suarez came very close to recognizing the negative character of these theorems when they called them hypothetical, i.e., 'if there is a triangle, then ...'.)

The theorems of descriptive psychology also exhibit a negative apodictic character; they all state it is impossible that a being mentally active in such and such a way, should not exhibit this or that property or relation. Thus according to our doctrine the thinking of certain concepts does not give rise simply to negative knowledge but to apodictically negative knowledge; consideration of concepts motivates the negative apodictic knowledge: 'such a thing *can* never be'. Those who oppose this doctrine and take axioms to be affirmative (e.g. the sum of the angles of all triangles equals two right angles) must say that their theorem refers to all 'existing' triangles, and 'existing' must include triangles 'existing in the future and the past'. In other words, they must pretend that something that does not exist exists! The other approach, which is used by Aloys Müller and Edmund Husserl, is to change the objects of mathematics into 'ideal objects' – which again amounts to resorting to fictions.

We have already had occasion to note that this discovery of Brentano's is of utmost importance. Nothing is more damning to the present condition of contemporary philosophical thought than the fact that it is not able to understand and appreciate this simple truth. In order to simplify their operations, mathematicians allow themselves the use of fictions, i.e., subtraction is reduced to the addition of so-called negative quantities. In a similar way, logicians resort to the fiction of treating a negative judgment as though it were a positive one and they affirm, not a thing, but the 'non-existence' of a thing; or they treat apodictic judgments as though they were perceptions of 'necessities' or 'impossibilities;' or they treat categorical judgments as if they were the comprehending of a 'being such-and-such' (*So-sein*) i.e. S being P. We cannot fail to see, however, that those who want to reduce all inner differences to the difference between facts affirmed are often wholly unaware that these reductions are merely artificial simplifying devices. On the contrary, they regard it as accurate psychological description (viz. Geyser in his book *Vom Kampfplatz der Logik*, Freiburg, 1926) or they feel they are making a genuine contribution to ontology (viz. Russell in his *Analysis of Mind*, London and New York, 1921). Cp. Brentano's doctrine of the fictitious character of all so-called *entia rationis* in his *Psychology*, and p. 103; cp. *The Origin of Our Knowledge of Right and Wrong*, Kraus's introduction.

9 Here Brentano is referring to his doctrine of synthetic (predicative) or double judgment, which he put alongside thetic judgments, simple assertions, and postulates. Thetic judgments take the form 'A is', or 'A is not', while the synthetic judgments have the form 'A is B', or 'A is not B'. Cp. *Psychology* and *The Origin of Our Knowledge of Right and Wrong*, and Marty, op. cit.

10 This doctrine is expounded in *The Origin of Our Knowledge of Right and*

Wrong. Cp. also Oskar Kraus, *Zur Theorie des Wertes; Eine Benthamstudie,* Halle, 1901, and 'Die Grundlagen der Werttheorie' in Frischeisen-Köhler's *Jahrbücher der Philosophie,* Berlin, 1914. The most advanced version of the doctrine appears in the new edition of *Origin.*

11 *The Origin of Our Knowledge of Right and Wrong* shows that those 'acts' which Brentano calls emotions that are experienced as being correct (*als richtig charaktisiert*), since they come from the concepts, exhibit a character which is analogous to apodictic knowledge. Cp. Kraus's introduction to *Origin,* especially Brentano's letter to Kraus in the Appendix.

12 A more detailed discussion of this theory of value and preference is to be found in *Origin* and in Kraus's 'Grundlagen der Werttheorie', *Jahrbücher der Philosophie,* Berlin, 1914; in the latter work Kraus still adheres to the correspondence theory, which he later came to reject.

13 The doctrine of direct and indirect modes of presentation (*modus rectus* and *modus obliquus*) is discussed in *Psychology,* Appendices and Introduction. As concerns the doctrine of temporal modes, cp. Part One, Chapter V, above; Part Two, Chapters II and III; and the appendix to the *Psychology.*

14 The continuity of qualitative differences is a continuity of relative local differences. Cp. Part One, Chapter V.

15 Cp. *Psychology,* p. 236 n.

16 Cp. note 11. That something, for example a cognition or joy, is 'good' simply means that we know that it is impossible for love (valuation) that is directed towards it to be unjustified, i.e. for it to contradict a justified love. The apperception of the justified emotional act, which originates in the concepts, leads to this axiomatic and negative-apodictic knowledge. Cp. *Origin,* op. cit. The emotional life is a new source for our cognitions and knowledge (for our value judgments and knowledge of value).

17 This was thoroughly discussed in Part One.

18 Here Brentano repeats what he stressed in the Appendix to the *Psychology.* Secondary consciousness always contains presenting and affirming, yet it does not always include emotional activity; this is to correct a doctrine expressed in the first edition of the *Psychology.*

19 Cp. pp. 25 and 106.

20 The text here reads 'whose presentation is an intuition' (*dessen Vorstellung eine Anschauung ist*). It should obviously be 'whose object is an intuition', and it means that some thinkers sometimes put the perception of conceptual activities in the category of intuition, while normally only the intuition of sense objects comes under the heading 'intuition'.

21 Ernst Mach, in particular, and some people influenced by him are guilty of this absurd identification.

22 Someone who sees and denies his secondary object (his act of seeing and his perception of this act of seeing) would err; this would not be true of a person who denies the primary object, i.e., the colour. The act of seeing exists, colours do not.

23 With regard to these comments on noetic and sensory objects we should bear the following in mind: As indicated in Kraus's footnotes to the *Psychology* and as pointed out in the Introduction thereto, the word 'object' has a synsemantic function in the expression 'to have something as object'.

The same, obviously, applies to the terms 'noetic and sensory object'. Brentano uses these terms as abstracta and abbreviations; he, more than anyone else, is entitled to use them in this way, for he has clearly pointed out their synsemantic character.

'I have something noetic or sensory as object' or 'I have a poetic object' means nothing but 'I am a sensory or noetic intellective being that presents'. There are only things, *Realitäten*, beings, and among these there are things or beings that present, judge, love or hate something (namely other things or beings). If I think of a triangle or something coloured in general, then I think, according to the text, of a 'noetic object'.

Yet it would be a complete misunderstanding of Brentano's teachings if we were to regard this grammatical name 'noetic object' as a logical name, i.e., if we were to assume the existence of 'noetic objects'.

Clarification of the situation is very difficult, if not impossible, as long as the negative character of axioms and apodictic truths is stubbornly contested. If theorems such as $2 + 1 = 3$ were affirmative, 'noetic or ideal objects' could only exist in Cloud-Cuckoo Land. If thinkers would finally realize that they are dealing with universal negative apodictic denials, then they could do away with this shadowy realm, countless books dealing with these fictions would not be written or printed, and people's energies and resources could be put to better use. Cp. Introductions to *Psychology* and to this volume, and, in particular, note 8 above.

24 In other words: what I intuit sensorily and have as my object falls into several classes.

25 'Concrete' but not individual!

26 This is the actual use of the word 'Gestalt'. Any other use must be merely a metaphorical one, and, for the most part, a misuse.

   Sounds are not restricted by shape (*gestaltliche Begrenzung*). Cp. note 31 below.

27 According to Brentano, we can only make the transition between specifically different colours via intermediary qualities.

28 It is interesting to note that according to Alfred Kastil, Brentano's methodology is strictly limited to that which is accessible to inner perception; he does not deal with the question to what extent differences in the physiological stimulus come into play. Naturally it can happen that one stimulus displaces another; in this case the phenomenon would be different.

   At this point an objection which was raised by Eisenmeier ('Brentano's Lehre von der Empfindung', *Monatshefte für Pädagogische Reform*, 1918) should be mentioned, namely that the investigation suffers from a *petitio principii*. For someone to arrive at the proposition that the analogy of lightness excludes a unity of species, it is necessary to have recognized the difference between certain species. As a matter of fact this is correct. Yet it is doubtful whether the accusation is justified. According to Kastil the situation is as follows: I do not need the criterion of the heterogeneity of various shades of lightness in order to recognize colour and sound heterogeneously, because in this case it is clear from the very beginning and everybody can easily recognize it. For this reason there has never been any conflict concerning the fact that a sound does not belong to the same species as a colour. Brentano has used the advantage and has taken from this clear situation a criterion which can be used to throw some light into the darkness that engulfs the other qualities and makes it so difficult to find order. This he did by starting from the assumption that it is easier to determine the differences in species of the element of lightness, and thus its analogy, than to determine the difference in species of the quality itself.

29 For this third species Brentano also uses the term '*Spürsinn*', (sense of feeling).

30 A more detailed discussion of this topic appears in Brentano's *Untersuchungen zur Sinnespsychologie* [Leipzig, 1907].

31 The term 'gestalt' is to be understood here in the original meaning of the word. It is a term which has to do with the concept of shape and its related, delimiting properties. We encounter things with shape both by means of visual and tactile sensations. The more unclear and undifferentiable the localization, the more difficult it is to discern the shape. In the acoustic realm there is no such thing as shape in the true sense of the word. The volume of one sound may be greater than that of another, yet it never appears as round, triangular or cubic. Thus it becomes necessary to limit the apparently general statement accordingly, as Brentano does below.

Brentano was in no way whatsoever referring to the figurative 'sound gestalt' – a very popular concept of modern Gestalt theory. According to Brentano, Ehrenfels's configurations of sound are by no means simple qualities of shape; they call for a special analysis which Brentano gives in *Untersuchungen zur Sinnespsychologie*. It is inadmissible to evade analysis by inventing fictitious new qualities which allegedly do not lend themselves to analysis.

32 According to Brentano, every sensory object has a local generic determination; soon after he finished the present essay he realized that phenomenal spatial things lack final specific determination. The relevant essay follows below, Part Two, Chapter III.

33 A more detailed investigation of the intensity is made in Brentano's *Untersuchung zur Sinnespsychologie*.

34 'These', i.e., the transcendent local relations, are not given in the sensory impressions; yet experience enables us to extract them from sensory impressions, and they constitute, from the practical point of view, the only interesting local data. Therefore we will devote ourselves not to the phenomenally given local determinations, but only to the transcendentally existing ones.

35 Professor Kastil notes: If the sounds, for example, were not original or if they were only localized analogously like colours, etc., then one could not call them mental phenomena in the same sense. They would be neither an example of something mental nor of something physical. Thus the adherents of this special empiricism would have to maintain that we can also sense something other than physical things.

36 The corrections pertaining to this paragraph are included in the sections on intuition and concepts below and in the Appendix to *Psychology*, nos. XII and XIII. Earlier Brentano believed that we intuit absolute final species; later, he came to regard this theory as false and he discarded it.

What does 'absolute species' mean? The concept is a negative one and means 'not merely relative differences'.

Between sensory qualities as such, for example, between colours as such or sounds as such there can exist nothing but qualitative differences. The qualities as such do not exhibit any local differences or relations. Therefore, from the very beginning, if we encounter local differences in intuition (sensations of colours or of tactile qualities), these differences of place must exist as such. Thus we must not only intuit something local (spatial) that exists in relative terms, but also something local that presents itself in absolute terms.

At an earlier period, and most likely also at the time the present essay was written, Brentano believed, as mentioned above, that we can also intuit locally absolute final species; even though this theory is dismissed as false, the fact remains that we intuit something local that is absolute (something with a spatial dimension) at least in a general sense, when we intuit sensorily qualified things next to each other – the reason being that every relative determination contains, in general, an absolute determination. Cp. p. 119, note 54.

But we know *a priori* that if something locally relative actually exists transcendentally, then there must also exist something locally absolute in general as well as *in specie specialissima*, because the existence of something undetermined, something universal, is an absurdity. This is overlooked by the relativity theorists.

37 The last sentence refers to transcendent spatial actuality and not to phenomenal localization. In the final absolute determination the latter is not given intuitively. Transcendent localizations must be determined to the very final species, yet they will always remain unknown to us. Cp. *Psychology*, Appendix, nos. XII and XIII.

38 I.e. in connection with intensity.

39 Cp. the essay on intensity in *Psychology*, Appendix No. VI, and additional material on the theory of intensity which allows for another concept of intensity in different qualities in addition to the concept of 'the density of the appearance in the sensory field'.

I would like to point out right here that the density of the appearance in the sensory field, that is to say, the density of that which appears, that which is sensed, must correspond to something like the density of the sensing itself, i.e. of the mental state. If we see something manifold and continuous, then this act of seeing is continual and multiple. We say 'multiple' because as beings who see something manifold and continuous, we do not become a multiplicity of continuous beings, we remain one unity with continuous and manifold qualities. For example, if we hear and see we remain one single thing, i.e., we do not become several different beings, but rather one being with a number of qualities. Cp. p. 106. Intensity of consciousness is thus to be understood as a certain multiplicity of appearance, if the intensity of that which appears is understood in terms of density in the phenomenal sensory field.

40 Cp. in this context the essay on Revesz's theory of sound in Brentano's *Untersuchungen zur Sinnespsychologie*. Revesz presented, somewhat later

than Brentano, a related analysis of the sensation of sound.

41 If the black/white scale were identical with the lightness scale, and if red had the lightness of grey without a specific lightness of its own, then red itself would have to be part of grey.

42 This conclusion originates in Brentano's theory of intensity, on p. 50, as well as in *Untersuchungen zur Sinnespsychologie*.

43 This sentence becomes clear if we look at a 'colour pyramid', for every degree of grey is located on the straight line that connects the two vertices. A certain red which is of the same lightness as a certain grey is located at a point outside this line. That means that the red is further away from the two vertices which mark the black/white line than the grey of the same degree of lightness.

44 With regard to this question cp. Eisenmeier's *Untersuchungen zur Helligkeitsfrage*, Halle, 1905 and 'Brentanos Lehre von der Empfindung' in *Monatshefte fur Pädagogische Reform*, Vienna, 1918. He maintains that Brentano has tried to find several solutions to the problem, among them the following: the lightness and darkness of a colour correspond to those of grey which contrasts with black and white to the same degree as the colour concerned.

45 This is also telling – as mentioned above (note 40) – against Revesz. The situation, however, is analogous in the realm of sound. There one must separate the tonal whiteness and tonal blackness of a sound from the specific degree of lightness, which is an attribute of sounds regardless of their pitch.

46 Location and quality are the elementary differences of sensory objects because intensity can be reduced to extent (*Extensität*). Lightness is an attribute of every quality, whether the quality is brightly coloured or unsaturated. The temporal sequence belongs in the area of the mode of presentation, i.e., the intuition of something mental. This point will be discussed in the next section.

47 As Brentano noticed, by saying that time is the form of inner sense, Kant touched upon something very important: it is true that we intuit something temporal that is absolute in general, in so far as we intuit something thing-like (regardless of whether it is physical or mental); however, we never intuit any absolute temporal species but only continually changing temporal modes (of our sensing), which appear to us as a whole. Several observations on this question follow below, as well as in *Psychology* and in my book *Franz Brentano*, Munich, 1919. Cp. in particular, Part One, Chapter V, section 5, section 10 above.

48 It should say 'every determination' instead. The area which we intuit is determined as to the third dimension only in so far as it is intuited as something which belongs to something three-dimensional, i.e., as a surface.

49 What does it mean to say the front surface is facing us? In the *Psychology*, the essay beginning on p. 311 says that we sense – in the visual intuition of space – the area which we intuit as something that is at a distance from an unqualified centre that we intuit *in modo recto*.

This essay dates from 21 November 1916 (not 1917 as it reads there). Yet it is hardly necessary to adopt this theory, according to which we intuit as point of reference something local that has no qualities; relative to this point of reference we localize the qualified area as something at an undetermined distance from it. I have the distinct impression that the above-stated opinion is nothing but a vestige of the doctrine of 'ego-centric localization' which Brentano himself rejects.

50 We are allowed to draw a parallel to the intuition of space because in both cases a boundary shows us that something belongs to a continuum (of three dimensions or one dimension). But with regard to the temporal intuition we encounter a one-dimensional direction of the course of time marked by 'before' and 'after'; while we have no such analogy as concerns spatial intuition, since in front and behind do not occur primarily and are reversible.

51 In his work on space and time, Anton Marty supports this view, which Brentano rightly rejects.

52 'Local determination' means 'determined with respect to location'; the two-dimensional area is determined in some way or other, although not *in specie* with regard to the third dimension because it is seen 'somewhere' although in an undetermined manner.

53 I.e., in the act of hearing.

54 I put the word 'absolute' in brackets since absolute local determinations *in specie* cannot be intuited, according to Brentano's definitive theory.

The certainty that the difference between good and bad localization does not stem from a higher or lower degree of absolute local determination is enhanced by the fact that absolute final local species (analogous to the final colour species red, blue, yellow, etc.) are not given at all in intuition; Brentano realized this only after he had finished this essay (cp. *Psychology*, pp. 311 ff and the last chapter of this volume).

Let us point out once more that we intuit something local-relative which includes the local-absolute only in general; an analogous phenomenon is the intuition of something larger and something smaller, i.e., of something that is relatively large and this intuition, the only one we can have, includes the intuition of something large in general. If this is true, then the presentation of the 'relative positions', the presentation of the local relations (of that which is locally relative), is not acquired by a comparison in the usual manner, as might be assumed on the basis of the text, but is an original relative act of presenting which is contained in the sensation itself.

We have an analogous situation in connection with temporal intuition (see Part One, Chapter V) in so far as it too contains something relative. The greater or lesser clarity of this relating act of presentation depends on physiological conditions.

As long as we adhere to Brentano's original doctrine – that we intuit absolute spatial species – we encounter almost insurmountable problems with regard to the perception of something that is spatially relative. It seems that the intuition of absolute spatial species would have to be completed by the intuition of other spatial relations, which we would acquire by means of special differentiations and comparisons. The knowledge, however, that we have no intuition whatsoever of absolute local species (nor of absolute temporal species) eliminates in a single stroke the apparent problem, because in a spatial and temporal relation our intuition is relative from the very beginning; it is produced by means of presentations *in modo recto* and *in modo obliquo*. Special comparisons come into play only when we are dealing with noticing and recognizing differences. A. Gelb's 'Theoretisches über Gestaltqualitäten', *Zeitschrift für Psychologie*, Vol. 58, 1910, touched upon this subject.

55 Here Brentano very decidedly rejects any intuition of unqualified places. This is also directed against the auxiliary assumption which was made later that there exists an unqualified place of reference for visual things; see *Psychology*, Appendix, pp. 363 f.

56 For more details see *Untersuchung zur Sinnespsychologie*.

57 It would be a newly added mode of thinking if we were to intuit absolute final local species (in the same way as we intuit absolute final colour species) and relate these to each other. Later on Brentano clearly emphasized that this is not the case, and he stressed that the relative mode of thinking is original.

The present essay shows, in my opinion, the transition from the old theory to the new, particularly in the paragraph where the intuition of local relations is attributed to the act of sensing itself, where it is related to the *modis obliquis*, and where abstract elements are denied.

58 In other words, this is not an act of presentation at which we arrive by means of generalization and abstraction, but this presenting of something relative ('relative thinking') is part of the sensing itself, it is an act of sensing, as pointed out below. The perception of shape (form) also falls under the heading of sensing.

A person who is unable to notice an act of presenting and judging in the act of sensing, i.e., an 'intentional character', will not be able to understand these remarks.

Professor Kastil writes in this connection:

It is not difficult to realize that the term which is introduced here, the term of the "relating act of sensation" is of importance for the question of the origin of the concept of number. Many things are originally intuited, and are not introduced into the objects of intuition by an act of thinking. This goes hand in hand with the most mature state of Brentano's metaphysics, where the difference between that which exists as the ultimate unity and that which manifests itself as a multitude is fundamental.

An interesting consequence of this theory of the relating act of sensing is that the act of sensing which, according to Brentano, is always also a blind act of belief in the primary object, constitutes such a belief not only in the sense of simple affirmation but also in the sense of attribution and even privation; without the latter it would be utterly impossible to make any differentiation at all. In contrast to the opinion that the sensing is nothing but a positive affirmation we can, therefore, say that sensation also contains negative elements. Obviously this is not to be understood in the sense that one can present something negative; it means that the sensation also contains a negation, insofar as we are not dealing with wholly non-differentiating sensation; one may well assume that such a thing does not exist at all.

59 This not only shows that Brentano attributed the concept of shape to animals, but it also reveals the processes that are necessary to render such a conception possible. Upon closer investigation we see that the sensing consciousness itself is a rather complicated state; and this analysis of the sensation, which reveals that sensation is not just a presenting consciousness but a judging, believing and differentiating consciousness as well, explains how a conception of shape can come about not only in human beings but also in animals. Even the inclusion of *modis obliquis* is unavoidable when we deal with differentiations.

60 This 'relating act of sensing' is an act of comparing, as a consequence of which we notice the 'particularity of the impression', i.e., the differentiating element.

61 Brentano believes that the presentation of something larger includes the presentation of something large; nevertheless the two presentations are not the same, i.e. the former has a different object. Thus we might believe that the confused presentation includes the distinct one, yet that it differs from the latter with regard to the object. Brentano, however, does not accept this parallel. In the case of a distinct act of presenting, nothing but new differentiating relations are added. These, however, fall within the realm of inner perception. In his *Allgemeine Erkenntnislehre*, Berlin, 1918, p. 135, Schlick opposes some of Stumpf's statements that relate to this; he says:

> If, on hearing a chord, we have a sensation of a harmonious entity in one case, while in another case we distinguish the individual notes, then this directly given structure, the chord we experience, is something different in each of the two cases; that which we experience in the former case is different from that which we experience in the latter.

This clearly shows that it is correct to say that the experiences differ in the two cases because the other experiences include the new differentiating relations, while the hearing of the chord, i.e., C-E-G, is included in both experiences. This is true not because the 'physical causes' are the same, but because we establish the hearing of the same notes and thus recognize that it is the same chord. The same is true of Helmholtz's analysis of sound.

Because the relating act of sensing itself must be regarded as an act of sensing (cp. p. 57) we can speak of different acts of sensing in the two cases concerned. The main question, however, remains whether or not the same sound qualities are sensed. In this context we must bear in mind that the accompanying feelings may be different in the case of a confused and a distinct act of hearing, which in turn will imply a different kind of 'experiencing'. From the terminological point of view it is incorrect to say that we experience sounds, colours, etc. We experience states of consciousness, i.e., the act of hearing sounds, the act of seeing something coloured. We do not experience something spatial or something coloured. Schlick's concluding sentence is worth noting, 'We must deny that there is a function that consists in the noticing of contents of consciousness. There simply is no inner perception.' People have spoken of a 'psychology without a soul', but a psychology without perceiving and noticing has never been mentioned before. Since this denial of perceiving and noticing functions obviously relates to functions of consciousness, it would be interesting to know how the critic arrived at his statement, how he knows, e.g., that the 'experiences are different in the two cases', when, according to his own doctrine, he is unable to notice and inwardly perceive anything?! Cp. however, Part One, Chapter IV, note 3.

62 The proof is given in the *Untersuchungen zur Sinnespsychologie.*

63 We must remember that this survey of descriptive psychology (phenomenal psychology) was originally intended as an introduction to metaphysics. All that remains of this introduction is the part that has been printed here. The question of 'spatial determination' follows below in Chapters II and III.

64 The 'sensory objects', in so far as they are mental, denote the sensory acts themselves, to the extent that they become the object of inner perception (of secondary consciousness) and, broadly speaking, the objects of noticing in the narrowest sense or in the sense of apperception.

65 In the realm which shows us mental sensory objects, or rather, where we have something sensory-mental as object, judgments are sometimes evident: according to Brentano the judgments of inner perception in the narrowest sense are evident ones, even if they relate to sensations and affects. On the other hand, not every differentiating judgment in this area is evident, for many deceptions occur.

66 A precise assessment seems to be impossible; inexact assessments, on the other hand, which establish clearly some differences without exactly indicating their quantity can be evident.

67 Namely to the sensory act of presenting.

68 Everything that we inwardly perceive or apperceive is mental and relates to something. It is indubitable that we never notice or perceive anything inwardly without intuiting something which mentally occupies itself with something else, something which mentally relates to something else, something which has something else as an object.

69 Cp. Part One, Chapter V, section 10.

70 We must not conclude from this phrase which Brentano uses that he believed that the dog judged, 'My master is not here'. All that is meant is that the dog makes a negative judgment in relation to something whose absence is bound up with feelings of displeasure.

71 As sensing being I am a judging being, i.e., usually a being that believes in something (qualitative-extended), a being that makes positive judgments. Yet the act of sensing is also accompanied by an act of differentiating, and in the latter sense I am not purely positive, I also make negative judgments. The knowledge that no intuition and no sensation shows us anything individual, and for this reason is in all cases universal because it does not provide us with final local and temporal species, is also of great importance for animal psychology.

72 Pleasure and pain are to be understood as meaning sensory pleasure and pain, or, in other words, pleasure and pain affects.

73 Stumpf's emotional sensations.

74 Cp. *Psychology*, pp. 144, 199.

75 Longing, fear, hope are complicated mental activities. Cp. *Psychology*, p. 236 n. 1.

To indicate it once more: in hope, the following things must be given: 1) a love for something; 2) a belief that that which one loves is likely to happen; 3) a satisfaction that that which one loves will most likely happen; 4) a sensory affect complex which is connected with this love and this knowledge. *Mutatis mutandis* in other cases of joy or sadness that something is or that something is not.

76 Obviously, I directly perceive my locationless sensation of something locally qualified while I perceive the locally qualified thing indirectly.

77 Cp. notes 16 and 18 to Part One, Chapter II.

78 One must not be afraid to point out the obvious. After all Brentano's statement in *Psychology*, where he says 'a landscape that I see' was interpreted to mean that one can see a landscape in the same way one can see red or blue. Cp. *Psychology*, p. 79 note 2.

Therefore I would like to stress here that Brentano does not mean that we can actually 'see' feet or heads. In this context, where we are concerned with the proof of the fact that one and the same subject sees a whole *Gestalt*, and that there could not be, consequently, many seeing beings where one sees one half and the other the other half, Brentano takes the liberty of using ordinary language. It would have been better to say, 'were there many seeing beings each of whom saw one third of a coloured form, then there would be no one who saw the entire form'.

79 Even if we perceive ourselves inwardly, we never perceive ourselves as individuals. All we know *a priori* is that we are a single entity and not a multitude, in so far as we know *a priori* that a perceiving being cannot be identical with several things perceived. Cp. *Psychology*, Appendices XII and XIII. In addition, the possibility of making comparison calls for a single subject, etc.

In my opinion, the mental nature of the subject of our consciousness follows from the knowledge that we are a single entity and not a multitude. Because even something like a point must coincide with some other point, and constitute, in a multiple manner, a boundary. Every point of any given continuum allows us to differentiate parts with regard to those sides of the point which form the inner boundary. This is already incompatible with the unity of our subject. If this subject is actually a single entity and not a multiple one, then it can have no extension and thus it cannot be something that has the character of a point, because there is no point that does not form the boundary of something extended.

80 Here I took the liberty of changing the text in a way which corresponds to Brentano's definitive belief, as expressed in *Psychology*, Appendix XVI (on *Ens Rationis*) and below.

81 It is important to note that the discussion here revolves around the continual character of the mental act, in particular the act of sensation. 1) The act of sensation appears as something continual (not as a spatial continuum, but as a continual-multiple) in so far as it exhibits a continuity of temporal modes, and, 2) in so far as it is directed toward something spatial. Any continual

multiplicity is one-dimensional, provided the time continuum is taken into consideration; it is three-dimensional (or belongs to the realm of the three-dimensional), if the sensation relates to something spatial.

82 Cp. above, Part One, Chapter V, the last section.

83 It is interesting to compare this statement with the *Psychology*, Appendix, pp. 311 ff and 362–3, concerning that which we intuit *in modo recto* during the act of seeing.

There, Brentano points out that we intuit *in modo recto* an unqualified place in general; while we intuit *in modo obliquo* the qualified area which is at a distance from this place. Brentano regards this unqualified, never-changing here as a parallel to the now which we inwardly perceive with the mode of the present and which, like the 'here' never exhibits any phenomenal change.

He also says, however, in the present text, 'We perceive ourselves inwardly (*in modo recto*) with a single temporal mode, the mode of the present, and this mode shows directly that it belongs to a one-dimensional continuum'. Cp. Chapters II and III.

Yet in the present essay Brentano does not use an unqualified here that we directly intuit as a parallel to this mode of the present, but the visual area itself is intuited. We intuit this visual area, a qualified area, directly (*in modo recto*), and the area appears immediately as part of something three-dimensional.

I consider this theory to be the correct one; the one put forth later represents no progress, in my opinion. In the one-dimensional continuum of the temporal modes, every single temporal mode appears to be forming part of something one-dimensional; in the phenomenal spatial continuum, however, something three-dimensional (an area) appears to be forming part of something three-dimensional. This fully suffices to explain all optical phenomena.

84 When I intuit something special *in modo recto* the area is presented (intuited); if I intuit something spatial *in modo obliquo*, then what I present is correspondingly three-dimensional. According to Brentano's theory, which was criticized in the preceding note, an unqualified place would be intuited *in modo recto* and the qualified area, as boundary of something three-dimensional would be intuited *in modo obliquo*, and this is intuited even more indirectly. ...

85 Brentano is here arguing against Marty's book *Raum und Zeit*, Halle, 1916.

86 This is to be understood as follows: Assuming Marty is right when he says that we intuit absolute final temporal determinations, nevertheless these phenomenal absolute temporal species would represent only a very limited span, since our intuition of time, like our field of vision, appears to be of a very limited nature. Analogous to spatial intuition, the absolute temporal species of which we have an intuition would always have to remain the same; out of the possible continuum of infinite temporal absolute determinations only an extremely short span would recurrently appear to us phenomenally. Thus it would be infinitely improbable that we would, at this very moment, intuit the factually actual absolute temporal species. This point can be discarded as soon as we are clear about the relative character of

our temporal intuition, i.e. as soon as we realize that we do not intuit absolute, final, temporal species.

Professor Kastil explains this section as follows:

> If we were to intuit the actually existing absolute temporal species, then these would always have to be new ones in inner perception because in actuality no point in time repeats itself. Inner experience, however, does not show that such a continuous change takes place from the very first moment of our existence onward. On the contrary, it seems that no present differs phenomenally from an earlier or later present. If this phenomenal point of the present, determined to the final species, were to present itself, the odds would be one to infinity that it would be identical with that point of time at which the actual temporal sequence of things has arrived so far. This point of time would, furthermore, lead to the absurd consequence that inner perception, the infallibility of which is established *a priori* [cp. pp. 6 and 94–5] would deceive us.

87 That means we might believe that we have an intuition of a period of time that goes back much farther.

88 We make assumptions concerning the temporal order of previous experiences, whereby the sequence of our associations acts as the point of reference for these assumptions. Other factors that come into play are intellectual estimations, approximating time comparisons, etc., none of which fall in the sensory realm.

89 This sentence seems to mean: If we maintain the belief that we intuit final, absolute local species – a belief which is untenable and which Brentano gave up, too – then it is dubious whether final local determinations can be objects of general concepts, as the final qualitative species actually can. We can think of something blue, something red, the note C in general. This is possible because the final qualitative species does not individualize. But if there were final local species in intuition, then we would intuit in them the individualizing elements, because the spatial element is the *principium individuationis*.

Consequently a determined local species could not be presented analogously to a colour species *in specie* without being presented in an individual manner; we could not think of it as we would think of something coloured, a thing, or a body, but only as we would think of Socrates, this human being. Section 5 of the next essay attests to the correctness of my interpretation of this section.

90 This opinion is maintained, above all, by Brentano himself.

91 We have already pointed out above (see, too, *Psychology*, p. 314) that the concept of something being individual is a synthetic one, and that none of our intuitions and sensations exhibit the element of individualization; thus it is not the problem of universal thinking, but that of individual thinking that needs to be solved. The concept of the individual can only be formed by means of the presentation of negations and attributive presentations *in obliquo*. After all, the concept of the one is already a negative concept; it means something that is not a multitude.

Our conviction that we are individual is an *a priori* one. It is not uncommon, however, for *a priori* convictions to be confused with intuitions.

92 The text continues 'that is, from such an intuition that is given anew, when I think of the general element'. (The words 'that is' are to be added mentally.) This whole sentence, however, must be eliminated in light of the later theory according to which the repetition of simple concepts does not require the repetition of the intuitions from which they originated. Marty had already taught this doctrine. Brentano at first adhered to the Aristotelian doctrine that we think all concepts in terms of phantasms.

At that point in the text where I left out the sentence, Brentano had already abandoned the old established doctrine in so far as he assumes, in connection with concept syntheses ('house', 'dog' are combinations of concepts), that only the elements of these concepts are thought by means of a repetition of the intuitions. Brentano finally drops even this rudimentary vestige of the Aristotelian doctrine, and he thus agrees with Marty's belief and with the results of *'Denkpsychologie'*. Cp. the next two chapters.

93 This is a point where *Sprachkritik* comes into play; its most important principles are discussed in the Appendix to the *Psychology*, and in the introduction thereto. Cp. also the writings on philosophy of language by Anton Marty and Otto Funke. The question with regard to the function of personifying terms such as 'state' and 'church' is particularly complicated.

94 In the text it says, 'relegated to the realm of psychology'. The present work was intended as a psychological introduction to metaphysics.

95 We must emphasize once more that when he says the issue is to establish the existence of intelligible objects, this was never meant to be taken literally – neither here not previously – nor to introduce a realm of 'ideal object', a Neo-Platonism! All that Brentano wanted to say was that it is important for him in this context to secure the existence of general ideas, of thinking in general concepts. Only a misunderstanding of the phrase could give rise to the doctrine of 'ideal objects'.

96 I have added the words 'sometimes'. The sentence means: intellective activities (e.g. conceptual presentation) are always simultaneously objects of secondary consciousness which is itself intellective with regard to intellective acts. In addition, however, it is possible to make an intellective act, for example, one's conceptual presentation, into a primary object by remembering, for example, that we have had this conceptual act of presentation, and in so remembering we present it.

97 This is the question of categories. Aristotle assumed that we arrive through generalizations at several highest universal concepts – concepts which are subsumed under no other concepts.

Brentano follows more the Platonic line of thought without, however, becoming a victim of Plato's hypostasization. According to Brentano, there is one highest universal concept which he calls the concept of the real, of being, of things. As opposed to Rehmke, 'thing' refers not only to physical things, but is equivalent to being. Cp. *Psychology*, Introduction and Appendix. The chapters that follow deal in greater detail with the problem of universals.

II A More Detailed Discussion of the Process of Abstraction and the Universal Nature of Perception and Sensation

1 This essay is dated 12 January 1915 and is entitled 'On Universals'.

2 The word 'universal' is not meaningful in and of itself; it is not a name but rather a synsemantic expression which acquires its meaning only when other words are added, e.g. 'someone who thinks of a universal'. Despite the apparently parallel syntax it cannot be interpreted as a parallel to 'someone who thinks of something red'. It means rather 'someone who thinks something in general', i.e., 'someone who thinks something that is not completely determined'. This kind of thinking contrasts with the kind of presenting in which a thing is thought of together with all its determinations.

3 As concerns the Aristotelian doctrine, cp. Brentano's earlier work on Aristotle, in particular *Aristotles und seine Weltanschauung* (1911).

4 In other words, neither inner perception in the narrowest sense (secondary consciousness) nor any evident apperception reveals our mental states in an individualized manner. Thus the question arises how, in spite of the lack of these individualizing determinations, we are able to recognize that our inner perception reveals only an individual, indeed that only an individual can exist. Cp. below and *Psychology*.

5 In other words, our intuitions are universal in a certain sense, due to the fact that they contain no absolute, final, temporal species. Yet usually two things which differ only with regard to temporal determination are not regarded as being different individuals, but rather as differing only temporally. For this reason Brentano speaks in another context of 'sub-individual' (*'unterindividuellen'*) differences when referring to temporal differences.

In any case, the prevailing doctrine that all intuitions reveal something absolutely determined is for this reason, wrong.

Soon after he dictated this Brentano realized that our sensory intuitions not only lack final temporal determination, as is true of all intuitions, but they lack final local determination as well. Cp. the following treatise and *Psychology*, Appendix.

6 The text contains the word 'only' before temporal determination. However, because Brentano soon realized that spatial intuition also lacks final specification, I put the word in brackets. I could also have said 'not only'. It should read: 'which lacks the most specialized temporal determination and the final local determination for full individuation'.

7 Even though sensory intuition lacks final temporal and spatial differences, it comes closer to individuation than any other general conceptual act of presentation which results from so-called abstraction.

8 The comments concerning the triangle and the circles drawn in the sand obviously apply to all drawn 'geometric figures' or forms. They also apply to all our artificially created models. We cannot successfully realize or intuit a straight line, a plane, a body formed by planes.

9 The italics are Kraus's and are meant to emphasize the importance of this statement.

10 The concept of a three-dimensional body can be thought without being present in a sensory intuition. Just as we construct the concept of something four-dimensional by means of composition and synthetic thought, it would be feasible for a being which only has intuitions of two-dimensional things to form the concept of something three-dimensional that existed in itself.

Brentano, however, does not believe that our concept of three-dimensional space, i.e., something three-dimensional existing in itself, not something which is just a border of something four or five dimensional, etc., was synthetically constructed in this manner, for we, as seeing beings, intuit the two-dimensional area as something which belongs 'somewhere', i.e., as something which forms part of an independent three-dimensional structure.

Again we must bear in mind that this statement refers only to the phenomenally given three-dimensional, and that we must separate this question from the question of whether or not the world in which we live as physical beings is three-dimensional or has more than three dimensions. The questions concerning the number of dimensions greater than three does not refer to the temporal dimension, which must, as primary continuum, form the basis for the spatial continuum in the same way as it must form the basis for any mental existence and any multi-dimensional continuum.

11 Intuition provides us directly with only certain very elementary concepts, the subsequent steps occur by means of synthesis (conceptual construction). See below, and elsewhere, e.g. *Versuch über die Erkenntnis*.

12 In the text it says 'point', yet there is no doubt that this word here stands for 'area' or 'patch'. After all, section 6 clearly stressed the claim that points cannot be intuitively differentiated. In any case, the concept of something red is not abstracted from the intuition of an independently existing red point. The word 'patch' is also used as an alternative to 'point'.

13 Brentano himself ventures to make this claim. Cp. p. 50.

14 A very noteworthy statement: it shows that the situation is just the opposite of that which it is usually assumed to be. The usual view is that our concept of something continual is a composite one, and the concept of the point is an element thereof. In reality, however, the latter is a synthetic concept and presupposes that of the continuum; this does not prevent us from recognizing *a priori* the impossibility of a continuum without boundaries and without coincidence of boundaries.

There seems to be an analogy between the way in which we acquire the concept of the number one and the way in which we acquire the concept of the point. In the former case, the concept of the many is the primary concept, in the latter case it is the concept of the multiple continuum.

On the fundamental importance of the (synthetic) concept of the straight line cp. Brentano, *Versuch über die Erkenntnis*, Leipzig, 1925.

15 An example of this process is given in the present paragraph. All these processes are necessary in the acquisition of the concept of the straight line, including inference, because the additional aspect concerning the position of every single point of the line is already an inference.

The distinction between presenting *in modo recto* and *in modo obliquo* is mentioned above several times, and is discussed both in the Introduction and in the Appendix to the *Psychology*. Any presentation of a boundary involves those *modi* because whenever I think directly of a boundary, I must think *in modo obliquo* of that of which it forms the boundary.

16 Brentano deals here with the formation of concepts only in so far as it involves the physical. It shows that even with concepts such as red, blue, straight lines, planes and points, complicated processes are involved.

As concerns the formation of concepts of the mental and in particular of facts of consciousness, you will find sufficient information in the preceding chapters.

While only very few basic concepts are abstracted directly from intuition in the physical and geometric realms – most of it being a matter of the construction of concepts in the above-mentioned sense – an incomparably larger number of intuitive concepts can be formed through perception and apperception in the realm of consciousness.

In his *Psychology*, pp. 315 ff, Brentano says that the concept of something red is an intuitive one. Yet if the concept of the 'ideal or pure red' is acquired in the above-mentioned manner, then we are dealing with a synthetic and not a purely intuitive concept.

17 Cp. pp. 67–8.

18 I have eliminated the rest of this paragraph, because Brentano is here still trying to uphold the old doctrine that any conceptual repetition requires an intuitive presentation, by means of arguments which essentially repeat what was said on pp. 63 and 125. As already pointed out, Brentano soon dropped this doctrine and adopted the one presented in the next chapter.

19 The proof is to be found in Part One, pp. 6 ff.

20 Brentano supplements this thought in a dictation dated 1 February 1915, 'Zur Lehre von der unmittelbaren tatsächlichen Evidenz', by stating,

It is in fact possible for us, after having perceived ourselves with evidence, to repeat this same presentation in which we perceive ourselves without affirming with evidence that which is presented. This being so, many things can correspond to it; in this respect, this presentation is no different from any other universal presentation. Thus it seems obvious that if a being could have direct evidence of something other than that with which it is identical, we would no longer recognize inner perception as the perception of a single, individual object, and hence we would no longer recognize it as inner perception.

21 Sensory intuition (sensation) not only lacks temporal determination, but final local determination as well. In accordance with this later and final doctrine of Brentano's, I substituted the phrase 'something is missing ... namely the characteristic. ...' for the phrase 'only one thing is missing' in the text.

22 In my opinion, we should add here 'if we had the intuition of temporal object differences'. In this context the time problem is not fully discussed and is mentioned only in connection with universals.

23 St Augustine, *Confessions*, Book XI, section 14, trans. R. S. Pine-Coffin, London, 1961.

24 The specific determination of the spatial in intuition is not a *final* specific determination. Cp. p. 83 f.

25 Brentano reasons as follows: Assuming we intuited absolute, final, temporal differences, i.e., we intuited a different 'now' at every moment, it would still remain undisputed and indubitable that 'temporal intuition' (Brentano speaks of 'proteraesthesis') involves only a limited span of time, analogous to the intuition of space which only extends over a limited spatial area, e.g., a limited phenomenal visual field.

In this phenomenal continuum of absolute time elements – this phenomenal time stretch – at most one single element, one single time determination could be called actual, as actual time is a continuous flow and exists at any given moment only according to this single moment (according to one single boundary). All other determinations of this intuited time-continuum would be non-existent; even more, they would be impossible. Yet this impossibility would have to be noticeable in some way.

26 Some writers such as Anton Marty in *Raum und Zeit* maintain that final specific temporal differences do appear to us in *external* intuition. Cp. the preceding note. If this were the case, then – according to Brentano – inner perception, too, would have to present final specific time differences to us in every 'now'. Because inner perception is infallible, the actual final species would have to be given here. Yet inner perception shows us only differences in experiences, it never reveals changing temporal absolute object determinations.

27 In his book on space and time Marty expressed the view that external perception reveals final temporal differences in objects, and that on the other hand, inner perception shows no temporal determinations. Brentano, however, reminds us that it is generally believed that mental things, too, are subject to temporal change.

If we arrived at a presentation of 'before and after' only on the basis of the intuition of most special (absolute) time determinations, then the inner perception of mental things, too, would have to exhibit such final differences. The fact that it does not and that we nevertheless acquire those time presentations, proves that such presentations can be acquired without the help of final absolute temporal species.

28 I.e., if the concept of something coloured were a relative one in the sense that it were the concept of a comparative relation, then it could never be repeated without the activity of comparing.

29 This is an *argumentum ad hominem*, directed only against those who teach that quality concepts are also relative.

30 In order to have presentations of spatial or temporal relations in general, it must be possible to be able, at least in general, to have absolute presentations of the spatial and the temporal.

31 As we speak of temporal distances and differences, it seems that, by analogy with colour differences, something absolute must be given in intuition, to which this difference is connected – hence the justified demand to show this absolute.

We can see (rather vaguely in this essay, but much more clearly in the following one) that that absolute, which is considered to be a necessity for any comparative determination, must be given in intuition only in a very general manner, while more special time determinations are given only as relative ones. Cp. *Psychology* pp. 363 f. and Part One, Chapter V in this volume.

32 With all so-called relative things we speak of the fundament and the terminus of the relation. If two spatially distant places exist, then both place A which I consider the fundament of the comparison, and place B, which is the terminus, exist. With things that are 'temporally distant' (in the case of a succession) it is different: if the fundament of the relation exists now, then that which is at a temporal distance from it cannot possibly exist, it is earlier or later than the now and thus belongs in the past or the future. Cp. Introduction to the *Psychology*.

33 The thought relation (the so-called intentional relation) is different from the temporal relation. If, for example, I think of or believe in Pegasus or something that is *a priori* possible, then only the fundament of this relation exists, e.g. I, as the being that thinks of Pegasus or something impossible and that perceives itself as thinking these things. Yet that which I present or that which I believe to be true, Pegasus or the impossible, does not exist in any sense. It is nowhere, not even 'in my mind'. That which I make the object of my thoughts that which I think, thus does not have to exist.

   In Brentano's opinion, the situation is quite different with regard to something past or future. Here we are inclined to speak of 'historic facts'. Yet it would be utterly wrong to ascribe to something past or something future a 'mode of existing'. This would be just as wrong as it would be to attribute an 'intentional or mental existence' to something that we think; yet this is quite frequently done. All statements concerning different modes of existing go back to different modes of presentation and judgment, to that which Brentano calls the mode of presentation and of thinking. The same holds true of 'historical facts'.

34 The apodictic mode of the judgment includes the assertoric one, i.e., if I think, 'something cannot be' then, somehow or other, I include the thought, 'it is not'. This does not apply to temporal modes.

35 Brentano wants to say that any presentation of a succession or of any change or motion includes the temporal mode.

36 '... which belongs to the content of the presentation of the temporal' means that in order to present something temporal, one must present it in a certain manner (with a certain mode) and these modal differences, and not differences in the object, are what differentiate our time-consciousness. Actually, there are no absolute object-differences given in the intuition of time; the temporal is presented in general together with every presentation of a thing – indeed the temporal and the thing seem to be one and the same – and what appear as temporal differences are differences in the modes of presentation with which we present and judge something temporal.

37 In other words, absolute temporal species, thing-like (*dingliche*) temporal differences are completely transcendent. That which is given absolutely, not relatively, is something temporal in general, yet in the intuition of rest and motion, change, succession of sounds, we intuit it with changing temporal modes; in inner perception, however, we intuit it with the *modus praesens*.

38 In other words, since we have no intuitive concepts (cp. *Psychology*) of absolute, final, temporal species, the question does not arise which intuitions

such a concept is abstracted from. The concept of temporal final species is a synthetic one, the elements of which are derived from different intuitions; from the intuition of time in general, the temporal modes, from analogy and negation.

39 'Elsewhere' refers to numerous individual investigations of space and time, some of which are mentioned in the *Psychology*, others in *Kantstudien*, vol. XXV, 1920, pp. 1–23 and in Kraus's *Franz Brentano*, Munich, 1919. See especially Brentano's *Philosophische Untersuchungen Zu Raum, Zeit und Kontinuum*, ed. Stephen Körner and Roderick M. Chisholm, Meiner Verlag, Hamburg, 1976.

III   The Knowledge of the Temporal Absolute and Its Species

1 The essay was originally entitled 'Zur Lehre von der inneren Wahrnehmung' and is dated 1 February 1915.

2 Inner perception, as demonstrated above, can only relate to the present; this is true in so far as inner perception is infallible as secondary consciousness. Cp. Part One, p. 6.

3 Concerning the concept of teleiosis, cp. Kraus's book on Brentano, p. 49; the concept is connected with the concept of the degree of variation.

4 This note is dated 7 March 1915 and is entitled 'Gegen die psychologischen Realisten'.

The thought is as follows: it is conceivable that a past note C permanently appears to have the same temporal distance from a present note D; the mental state of that which, so to speak, appears as past would continue permanently.

Yet it is impossible that this appearance shows us something true, because the past actually recedes further and further into the past.

5 In other words, the infinitesimal temporal differentiation follows *a priori* from the boundary concept which we get from inner perception; a continual differentiation of the act of experience does not follow from it, however. Cp. section 4.

6 I.e. that there is no such consciousness of the continued existence.

7 An unchanged temporal persistence of a thought would be the persistence of the act of thinking in 'full teleiosis', the greater the change the smaller the teleiosis. Physical rest is a state in which the body persists in full teleiosis, the faster the movement the smaller the teleiosis.

8 With regard to this question cp. pp. 28 ff.

These deliberations and the following observations reveal that according to Brentano, we do not acquire the concept of time only from the temporal modes of the act of sensing, but rather the temporal, as such, is already present in inner perception in general as the concept of the temporal boundary; the specific differences, however, remain completely transcendent to us, and their existence, which is continual, can only be deduced from this boundary concept and is relative to it.

Just as we find the concept of the spatial absolute included in the concept of the spatial relative, the concept of the temporal absolute is included in the concept of the temporal relative. We encounter this concept both in inner perception, where we see ourselves as a temporal boundary, and in external perception, i.e., in sensation, provided it shows us things. Because, as the following elaboration shows, the concept of a thing is identical with the concept of time; that is, to say every thing presents itself as a temporal boundary, i.e., is temporally relative with regard to something else.

We must bear in mind that the 'absolute' does not include a denial of the relative; the absolute is an indispensable foundation for the relative.

According to Brentano, therefore, the intuition of the temporal modes of sensation, which is provided by the presentation of the present, the earlier and even earlier past, etc., is supplemented by the intuition of the absolute temporal itself; this, of course, occurs only in the most general terms as something like a temporal boundary which calls for a temporal continuity of before and after (obviously it can possess both). Thus the temporal concept of something earlier and something later would be given in connection with the modes. Brentano's objection against Marty's *Raum und Zeit* remains valid in so far as Brentano denies the intuition of specific absolute time differences; his objection seems to be less fervent, however, in other respects, as the intuition of the temporal absolute is taught, *in genere*, but not *in specie*.

It is very instructive to study Marty's book on space and time and to compare it with Brentano's doctrines. Perhaps it is not superfluous to point out that temporal determinations are attributed to things themselves according to Brentano. Things are simultaneous if they have the same specific temporal determinations, just as two things are the same colour if they belong to the same specific colour species.

IV   Further Investigation of the Universality of All Intuitions – In Particular Spatial and Temporal Intuitions and the Temporal Absolute Universals

1 Brentano dictated this essay in June, 1916. The thought that our inner and external intuition never shows us absolute substantial determinations differentiated in a final specific manner is expressed here in conclusion in a very general way. I published another similar treatise by Brentano in the Appendix to the *Psychology*, No. XII.

2 The expression 'directed towards universal objects' may be misunderstood. All that Brentano wants to say is that we think something (a thing) without thinking it as something completely determined.

Cp. my repeated notes in *Psychology* concerning the merely synsemantic expression 'object'.

3 'Undetermined' thinking is not a special mode of thinking. The mode of thinking does not change if at one time I think of something green here and at another time of something coloured. Brentano does not conceive generalizing thinking as a special mode of thinking. Therefore, I altered the text which said 'think in an undetermined manner'. (*'in der Weise unbestimmt denken'*), and said instead 'think ... in such a general way' (*'derart unbestimmt denken'*) in order to avoid misunderstandings.

4 It would be a contradiction to assume that colour is a logical part of all things that are coloured. Many things would have one part in common.

5 Marty (*Untersuchungen*, Halle, 1908) and those who study psychology of thought have arrived at the same results and maintain that something universal can be thought in the repetition of a concept without there being 'phantasma'.

6 According to Brentano's doctrine, the abstraction process never begins with something 'individual', because we never intuit anything individual. This is the reason why I put the words 'or something individual' in parentheses.

7 If we were to perceive ourselves inwardly as something material, physical, then there would be no cause for a dispute concerning the question whether the subject of the act of thinking is something physical or something non-physical. The same would hold true if we were to perceive ourselves in inner perception as mental subjects. Actually, however, we comprehend ourselves as neither one; we see ourselves simply as things (beings) who think, judge, love and hate, but we do not perceive ourselves as either physical or spiritual beings. The question concerning the physical or mental nature of the subject of consciousness (the soul) cannot be directly decided on the basis of perception, but only deductively, for example, on the basis of the comprehensive, unitary apperception of simultaneous states of consciousness. Cp. p. 123.

8 The mental acts (seeing, hearing, thinking) are accidents which include the substance as a part; the accidents are specialized indeed, but are free of any individuation, for this can only be attributed to the substance. Even though it is an attribute of substance, it is not given intuitively.

9 Here I have inserted the word 'final'. It went without saying for Brentano that we cannot think relative determinations, without at the same time thinking absolute ones, even if only in the most general manner. His example: the thought of someone who is richer than someone else, includes the absolute thought of someone rich in general. 'Absolute' means 'not relative'. Cp. section 11.

10 If intuition were to show us absolute places in final *specie*, we still would not know if and where these local species which we intuit are realized in actuality. Places would be shown to us that exist or can exist at tremendous distances from the place which our body occupies. If we intuit only relative (local) species, then we escape this peculiar result.

11 That which is not determined *in specie specialissima* is not completely determined, i.e. is universal, whether we are dealing with substances or accidents.

12 I have inserted the words 'or external ... respectively', since they seem to have been left out by mistake.

13 I have inserted the word 'continuum'.

14 No matter how much Brentano upheld his theory that only something present can be thought of *in modo recto*, while something past as such can be presented only *in modo obliquo*, he considered it an unsatisfactory solution to resort to the continuum of modes of presentation to replace the missing continuum of absolute temporal species in order to avoid certain difficulties.

These difficulties arise because temporal distances, that is, relative time species, are to be presented *in specie*; due to their nature, however, these time species would have to be connected with differences in absolute time position; yet it is said that we do not have a presentation of the latter. The actual solution is as follows: first we present temporal distances *in specie* only in so far as we present something that has the same temporal distance from something else as compared to a third temporal distance, or the distance is twice or three times as large, etc. Second, it is not correct to say that our relative temporal determinations include no absolute temporal position whatsoever; all that is correct is that we can present this element of absolute temporal position only in an undetermined manner, i.e., we cannot present it in a certain specific but only in a generic temporal determination. In other words, we do have an absolute concept of time, but only in a general sense; we do not have intuitive concepts of different final temporal species. The former, however, suffices to make possible both the conceptual as well as the intuitive presentation of relative time differences. This applies analogously to our presentation of space in connection with which the same difficulties would arise which Brentano, as already pointed out, noticed in the course of his investigations concerning the transcendence of local absolute specific determinations.

In an essay entitled 'Zur Lehre von der Zeit' (date unknown) it says that the transcendent time concept, i.e., the concept of the temporal absolute, is included in its generality in the concept of the real (the thing). It is a logical consequence that this concept is also given as the concept of a continuum, of something which includes an infinite number of transcendent time differences. Furthermore, however, nothing is given intuitively. In particular, we have no intuition of absolute determined specific transcendent temporal determinations whatsoever. In an essay dated 13 February 1915, it says that inner perception is completely limited to a single now, that it offers with certainty a boundary as being present, but a boundary characterized by the fact that it forms the boundary of a continuum which is bounded by it; in the temporal realm, this continuum can only be thought as something earlier or later, or as something earlier as well as something later. 'Despite the fact that inner perception is limited to one point, we not only present and affirm the point *in modo recto*, we also present and affirm a time span of which the point forms a boundary *in modo obliquo*.' Yet this time span is presented only in general and in a completely undetermined manner. Cp. also Part One, Chapter II, section 2.

15 The temporal beginning and the temporal ending exist in semi-plerosis (fullness), that which continues on exists in full plerosis.
16 A past or future point in time neither is, nor can it be; the present temporal determination, the present point in time is a differentiated point in time only in so far as it is distinguished from something that is not or cannot be.

INDEX

137

Index